5

conversations

you **must** have with

your son

THE BIBLE STUDY

Vicki Courtney

LifeWay Press®
Nashville, Tennessee

Published by LifeWay Press® Copyright © 2011 Vicki Courtney

This resource is based on the book 5 Conversations You Must Have with Your Son ©2011 by Vicki Courtney. Published in association with the literary agency of Alive Communications, Inc., 7680 Goddard Street, Suite 200, Colorado Springs, CO 80920 www.alivecommunications.com

ISBN: 9781415869574
Item: 005342724

Dewey Decimal Classification: 248.842
Subject Headings: MOTHERS AND SONS \ BOYS \ CHRISTIAN LIFE

To order additional copies of this resource, write to LifeWay Church Resources Customer Service, One LifeWay Plaza, Nashville TN 37234-0113; fax (615) 251-5933; phone toll free (800) 458-2772; order online at www.lifeway.com; e-mail orderentry@lifeway.com; or visit the LifeWay Christian Store serving you.

Printed in the United States of America

Leadership and Adult Publishing
LifeWay Church Resources
One LifeWay Plaza
Nashville, TN 37234-0175

CONTENTS

ACKNOWLEDGMENTS

Keith, in the process of writing this study, I was struck with how purposeful you have been in training and discipling our sons over the years. Our sons (and daughter) are so very blessed to have you for a dad. And I am even more blessed to have you for my own. Let the empty-nest years begin!

Memaw, how can I not include you in the acknowledgments, given the influence you have been in your son/my husband's life? I have reaped the benefits over the years as a result of your godly mothering. I love you!

Ryan and Hayden, as I type these very words, one of you is a week shy of getting married and the other, a week and a half shy of walking across the stage at your high-school graduation. By the time this study hits the shelves, you will be… on your own! (Gulp.) Thank you for the homemade Mother's Day cards you make me every year, for dancing with me to oldies music, and, most of all, for telling me you love me for absolutely no reason at all. I love you so much and can't wait to see what God has in store for your future.

Matt, I've said it before and I'll say it again: You are exactly what Paige's dad and I pictured when we prayed for our daughter's future spouse. My daughter got the "top-shelf kinda guy" she always dreamed about. Welcome to the family, son!

Lee, you are the best agent on the planet. I can't imagine where I'd be today had you not agreed to represent me back in 2005. Thanks for not just being an agent, but also a friend.

Pam Case, Sharon Roberts, Amy Lowe, Bethany McShurley, Rick Simms, April Dace, Jon Rodda, and the entire team on this project—I am grateful for your sincere desire to see needs met, lives changed, and, most of all, God glorified.

And acknowledgments would not be complete without giving thanks to the One who enables me to write, speak, live, breathe, and love. I pray this book will bring glory and honor to my Savior, Jesus Christ. I will never cease to be amazed that You use me in any capacity in Your kingdom purposes.

ABOUT THE AUTHOR

Vicki Courtney is an author and speaker whose ministry reaches more than 150,000 teens and tweens and their mothers each year. A mother of three children herself, she seeks to provide tweens, teens, and their parents with the tools necessary to navigate today's promiscuous culture.

She has conducted hundreds of radio and newspaper interviews and appeared on "CNN," "Fox News," and "CNN Headline News" as a youth culture commentator to address various issues impacting tweens and teens.

Vicki is a national speaker to women of all ages and the best-selling author of numerous books and Bible studies including 5 *Conversations You Must Have With Your Daughter*, 5 *Conversations You Must Have With Your Son* (trade version), *Your Girl*, *Your Boy*, *The Virtuous Woman*, and the popular series of magabooks for tween and teen girls, *Between* and *TeenVirtue*. Vicki is a two-time ECPA Christian Book Award winner and her book 5 *Conversations You Must Have With Your Daughter* is the recipient of a Mom's Choice Award.

A recent empty-nester, Vicki resides in Austin, Texas, with her husband, Keith. She is hopelessly addicted to Starbucks® Grande Skinny Vanilla Lattes, running, shoe shopping, and, most of all, spending time with her family. She is also quite fond of her two pint-sized Yorkshire terriers, Lexie and Scout, who she claims are the additional children her husband refused to have. You may visit Vicki at *www.vickicourtney.com* for more information.

Bethany McShurley, leader guide writer, is a freelance editor/writer who specializes in Christian curriculum and new author development. She hopes to spread the message that a relationship with Jesus can radically transform every aspect of life. Bethany resides in Maryland with her husband, Jon, and two sons.

VICKI'S LIVING ROOM FRIENDS

One benefit of any Bible study is the support and sharing that come from participating together. You'll enjoy getting to know the women in Vicki's DVD small group. See if you can find yourself in their words, experiences, questions, and joys of parenting boys.

Seated: Regina Gibson; Standing left to right: Shelley Bussell, Lori Apon, Leslie Alger, and Vicki

REGINA GIBSON, Nashville, TN
Regina and husband Chris have a busy household that just got busier. Micah Thomas, almost 2, just became a big brother to sister Hayley Elizabeth.

Regina describes Micah as "all boy" and full of joy! He's super active, quite adventurous, with a kind streak that makes one smile. "I desire to teach Micah to love the Lord and whole-heartedly pursue Jesus from his youth. It is helpful to see seasoned moms do this with intentionality in a culture that is drowning in the currents of worldliness. I think Vicki's study will aid in that effort.

"As a stay-at-home wife and mother I rejoice to serve my husband and children! I enjoy teaching God's Word on a regular basis in my church and in women's conferences."

SHELLEY BUSSELL, Nashville, TN
Shelley and husband Steve have three sons: Benjamin, age 9; Noel, 6; and Wright, 4. Shelley is a stay-at-home mom with Wright. She volunteers in her church's girls ministry and teaches

freshmen Sunday School and girls Bible study on Sunday nights.

What situations are you relieved you've made it through? "Having three active boys under the age of 5 and moving through that stage sometimes in tears and other times with laughter!"

Benjamin is "sweet spirited with an obedient heart. Noel loves to make us laugh and adores his brothers. Wright likes to keep up with his brothers and has a strong will that keeps me busy! I love my boys and life is always an adventure."

LESLIE ALGER, Austin, TX

Leslie is a CPA "on a 16-year break" as a stay-at-home mom, substitute teacher, and children's worker in her church. She and her husband, John, have three sons: Justin, age 16; Andre, 15; and Jacob, 14.

"Justin's name means 'full of justice,' which fits him perfectly! He is a great role model to his brothers. Andre brings great joy to the family; he is a gifted athlete with a generous and caring heart. With great confidence, Jacob uses his gift of teaching to lead the Fellowship of Christian Athletes group at school."

Leslie treasures dialogue with each son through nightly prayers. She enjoys writing in a special journal for each son.

LORI APON, Woodstock, GA

A widowed mother of eight, she became a grandmother this year. Lori homeschools and teaches a Sunday School class for widows. Son Brandon attends college while these sons live at home: Isaac, age 17; Evan, 16; and Micah, 13.

She describes Isaac as extremely tenderhearted and a servant. "Fun-loving and energetic," Evan is sensitive to the needs of others. A leader, Micah is "easy-going and looks for the best in all situations. He compassionately serves the homeless in our community." The hardest stage for Lori as a mom is when a son "bursts into manhood."

Lori loves studying God's Word. Digital scrapbooking and blogging (*www.aponhodgepodge.blogspot.com*) are her pastimes.

She shares a bonus DVD segment about ministry as a single mom. Follow Lori at *www.loriaponwidow.blogspot.com* to find out more about this ministry.

Our prayer is that you will look back to your 5 Conversations study as a marker in your own growth as a godly woman and mother.

ABOUT THIS STUDY

 This study is a companion resource to Vicki's *5 Conversations You Must Have with Your Daughter: The Bible Study*, published in 2009. (You can do this Bible study without having done the other, of course!) Almost immediately after 5 Conversations Daughter released, Vicki began to hear, "When will you provide something similar for moms of boys?" The research, cultural issues, and biblical principles justified such a study, and she began to pray and write.

In addition to her trade book releasing June 2011 (B&H Publishing), she developed the Bible study that is the basis of your experience. This six-session Bible study, for moms of sons from the cradle to college, is built around five conversations that should be ongoing in boys' formative years.

Conversation 1: "Don't define manhood by the culture's wimpy standards."

Conversation 2: "What you don't learn to conquer may become your master."

Conversation 3: "Not everyone's doing it!" (And other truths about sex you won't hear in the locker room.)

Conversation 4: "Boyhood is only for a season. P.S. It's time to grow up!"

Conversation 5: "Godly men are in short supply—dare to become one!"

In her DVD, Vicki introduces concepts moms will interact with during the week. Session 1 introduces the study and launches Conversation 1; sessions 2-5 set the context for the corresponding conversations; and session 6 challenges you to keep conversations going. Vicki's frequent use of statistics, trends, and research expose cultural lies for moms and sons seeking God's ways in a culture that often leads otherwise. These features are part of your workbook:

Let's Talk introduces new concepts.

Personal Reflection asks a mom to consider her own stance on an issue.

God's Take on the Issue reveals what the Bible has to say on a topic.

Conversation Boosters provide practical ideas (and some practice) on how to start important discussions with her son in age-appropriate ways.

Bringing It Home and/or **Wrapping It Up** helps moms apply concepts to daily life and bring a week to conclusion. Most groups will benefit from having at least 75 minutes for each session. The facilitator can customize ideas on pages 164-71. A leader kit (item 005342723), with one member book and two DVDs, is available. Vicki's teaching segments are 25 to 30 minutes each. Bonus and promotional footage are also included.

INTRO AND CONVERSATION 1

"Don't define manhood by the culture's wimpy standards. It's OK to be a man!"

Manhood is suffering an _____ _____.

Even secular media is asking, What's going on with our men?

Three truths give us the biblical foundation for manhood.

GENESIS 1:25-31
1. God created man in His image (v. 26).
Image = *tselem*, tseh´-lem; to "shade or _____"
_____ _____ _____.

2. Male and female, He created them (v. 27).

3. God gave man the charge to subdue the earth (v. 28).
Subdue = *kâbash*, kaw-bash´; to "conquer, subjugate, bring into bondage"

How do we temper our sons' natural energy and aggression without stifling their inner warrior?

Jesus gives us the perfect balance of _____ tempered with _____.

CONVERSATION STARTERS with your group:

Share some examples you are seeing of your son's (1) emerging manhood and/or (2) his expressions of tenderness.

Interested in reviewing this or other 5 Conversations Bible study sessions? You can download all digital sessions by going to www.lifeway.com/women

VIDEO GUIDE

SESSION1

WEEK 1

Redefining Manhood

Spanish Proverb

~

"An ounce of mother is worth a ton of priest."

SHAPING A DESTINY

let's talk **In my upstairs hallway, the walls are lined with portraits of my children. One of my favorite pictures is of my oldest son at age four; he's dressed in his dad's oversized blue button-down dress shirt. The sleeves are rolled up and a red printed tie hangs loosely around his neck. He sits on his dad's leather briefcase and rests his chin in his chubby hands. The hem of the shirt falls around his bare feet. The photo captures a little boy with dreams of growing up to be just like his dad.**

"Don't wait to make your son a great man— make him a great boy."
~Author Unknown

I loved the portrait so much that I had another one taken of him wearing the same outfit two years later, at the age of six. When he was eight, he agreed to another photo in dad's dress shirt provided I let him wear slacks this time! The last portrait taken in the "blue dress shirt" series was at the age of 12. My son was a preteen on the cusp of being a teenager, yet he still looked more like a boy than a man.

Once I planned to capture his image every few years until he fully grew into his dad's shirt. But when it wasn't as easy to get him back to the studio after the age of 12, my series stopped before his teen years. When I last stopped to look at the series of four pictures, tears filled my eyes.

That same little boy wearing his dad's work shirt with the sleeves rolled up is now 22 years old, a recent college graduate, and engaged to be married. (He's also now two inches taller than his dad!)

As I studied the pictures hanging side by side, I couldn't help but smile at his amazing journey. I count it an awesome privilege to play any part in shaping my son's life as he traveled the road to manhood. And for the record, I made an appeal for one last picture to complete the series before he began his new job. He is already putting that business degree to use by wisely requiring a "modeling fee" as compensation. Clearly, the days of bribing him with a Happy Meal® from McDonalds® are long gone!

Eighteenth-century hymn writer E. W. Caswell has said, "The mother, more than any other, affects the moral and spiritual part of the children's character. She is their constant companion and teacher in formative years. The child is ever imitating and assimilating the mother's nature. It is only in after life that men gaze backward and behold how a mother's hand and heart of love molded their young lives and shaped their destiny."[1]

PERSONAL reflection

Consider your son's destiny. What hopes and dreams do you have for his future? *Man of God, Respectful, servant to others, brings joy to others*

When you picture him as a grown man, what qualities do you hope you will see? *Love, respect, kind, helpful hardworking, joyful servant*

GOD'S TAKE on the issue

While much emphasis rests on the important role fathers play in the lives of their sons, the Bible clarifies that mothers also play a vital role in shaping the destinies of their boys. In the Book of 2 Kings, a time line shows the ruling kings of Israel and Judah and includes a brief description of each reign.

Look up the following groups of verses.

GROUP 1:   GROUP 2:

2 Kings 8:25-27   2 Kings 11:21-12:2

2 Kings 21:1-2   2 Kings 14:1-3; 2 Kings 15:1-3

2 Kings 21:19-20   2 Kings 18:1-3

What noteworthy legacy did these kings share?

Put a check beside common factors found in all of the verses.

✓ The king's name

___ The king's annual income and total net worth

___ The king's age at the time he began his reign

✓ The number of years he reigned

___ A resume of the king's previous leadership positions

✓ The name of the king's mother

___ The king's SAT score and class rank

In addition to a king's name and length of service, each passage includes the name of the king's mother. What significance might we draw from this? *We influence the legacy of the next generation*

Stop for a minute and recall your own family tree. Now imagine that beside the name of every male, the mother's name was included and the son's legacy was summed up with one of two phrases: "He did what was good in the eyes of the LORD," or "He did what was evil in the eyes of the LORD."

I am certainly not suggesting that mothers are to blame should their adult children choose to stray from God's path. I know plenty of godly mothers who, despite their devotion to the spiritual training of their children, have experienced the heartbreak of one or more of their children choosing the prodigal way.

As mothers, we play a part in shaping the spiritual destinies of our children; but in the end, we are not responsible for the finished product. Our children, just like us, are works in progress.

Write Proverbs 22:6 in this space.

Start children off on the way they should go, and even when they are old they will not turn from it.

The Message states it this way: "Point your kids in the right direction—when they're old they won't be lost." Our job is to provide our sons with a map and to point them in the right direction on the road to manhood. While we cannot make them into godly men, we can and should influence them.

PERSONAL reflection

Think about your earlier answers concerning your hopes for your son's future (p. 12). Circle here whether your list of dreams tends to be *more worldly focused or more spiritually focused.*

If you found yourself answering "more worldly focused," you aren't alone. Most of us spend a lot of time and energy hoping our sons will grow in athletic ability, excel in their studies, marry the perfect girl, and eventually enjoy large bank accounts. Yet we need to remember that God has bigger plans for our boys.

In the next reading we'll focus on a king who can teach us much when it comes to understanding biblical manhood. His story offers mothers a template on how to be spiritually focused when it comes to rearing our sons into godly men.

LIKE FATHER, NOT ALWAYS LIKE SON

let's talk **Josiah was a king who had his priorities in the right order. His reign serves as a positive example when it comes to the spiritual character we hope to cultivate in our sons' lives.**

"One father is more than a hundred schoolmasters."[2]

- George Herbert

GOD'S TAKE on the issue

Read 2 Kings 22:1-2. How old was Josiah when he became king?

Now write out verse 2.

When was the last time you were around a group of eight-year-old boys? Last I checked, eight-year-olds build plastic castles with Lego® sets, not real-life kingdoms. Clearly Josiah acted under the influence of wise adult guidance, but who pointed this lad in the right direction? More importantly, who encouraged him to do "what was right in the LORD's sight"?

While verse 2 (NIV) says Josiah "walked in all the ways of his father David," it's important to note that the word *father* is used figuratively, as in "ancestor" (HCSB). Josiah's actual father was King Amon, who preceded him on the throne.

Read 2 Kings 21:19-24 to get a history lesson on Josiah's biological father. Which of the following best describes King Amon?

● Good   ● Evil   ● It's a toss-up

A quick look at Grandpa's bio (Amon's father) proves interesting too.

Read 2 Kings 21:1-11. Which of the following best describes King Manasseh?

● Good   ● Evil   ● It's a toss-up

Comparatively speaking, how evil was Manasseh (v. 11)?

In addition to his long list of evils, what other abomination did he commit (v. 16)?

In the latter part of his reign, Manasseh was captured, bound in bronze chains, and taken to Babylon. It was then that he turned back to God and asked for His favor. Moved by his plea, the Lord listened and returned him to Jerusalem (2 Chron. 33:9-13). But while Josiah's grandfather may have eventually come to his senses, his father, Amon, did not.

Read 2 Chronicles 33:21-24, and check all statements that describe Amon's reign.

_____ He sacrificed to the images his father had made and served them.

_____ He made a 90-foot tall golden statue and demanded the people bow down and worship it each day.

_____ He did not humble himself before the Lord and incurred even greater guilt.

_____ He made little Josiah a coat of many colors to wear in the winter.

_____ His servants conspired against him and put him to death in his home after a two-year reign.

We can only begin to imagine the evil Josiah was exposed to during his father's rule. But cruel or not, Amon was still Josiah's father. A father's death—much less one that was the result of a plotted murder by servants in his own home—would land most boys in a counselor's office. Josiah had many strikes against him, yet by God's merciful hand, he prevailed in the face of adversity.

Read 2 Chronicles 34:3. What important decision did Josiah make at age 16, eight years into his reign?

In his twelfth year of rule, Josiah was 20. What action did he take at this time?

Second Chronicles 34:4-7 explains how Josiah literally traveled the nation, destroying altars to pagan gods. One Bible commentary said about the young king: "Josiah is the most astonishing instance that is contained in Scripture of goodness springing up, and attaining high perfection under the most extraordinarily unfavorable circumstances."[3] In spite of culture's moral decay and the godless example set by his immediate fathers, Josiah chose to pursue God.

What hope might Josiah's experience offer a mother who is rearing a son without a godly role model?

If you are not facing this situation, chances are you know a mother who is. Pause for a minute and pray for moms you may know who face this challenge.

We cannot be certain that Josiah's mother was a primary influence in shaping his spiritual destiny, but one Bible commentary notes:

> "God's providence seems to have watched over Josiah, and to have caused some care to be taken to guide the young king right. The queen-mother, Jedidah ("the beloved of God"), daughter of Adaiah ("the honoured of God"), may perhaps have deserved her lofty name, and given her boy the priceless benefit of a godly mother's example and counsels."[4]

The author speculates that King Josiah's mother may have acted as "regent"—or head of state—in his minority years, working to surround him with other godly role models throughout his reign.

PERSONAL reflection

Regents rule for a young royal until he or she grows old enough to manage alone.

List ways you serve as regent for your son.

What might he gain from observing your example?

In a sense, we are providentially assigned as "regents" in the lives of our young sons. We work hard to introduce them to God and to nudge them along His path, pointing out the blessings and benefits of being His child. In the back of our minds, we know a day is coming when we must let go of their hands and completely entrust them to God.

Like Josiah, our sons are growing up in a culture where the lines of morality have been blurred and godlessness prevails. Our tendency is to read about the sin and debauchery present in Old Testament times and conclude that it was far more evil than anything we've witnessed in our day, but the Internet alone contains a Pandora's box of evil that would likely make the idol-worshiping, pleasure-seeking Israelites blush.

Take, for example, the story a mom shared about a group of third-grade boys at a small private school. A teacher caught them passing around a wireless mp3 player during lunchtime and took up the device. Unfortunately, the boys weren't listening to music—they were watching hardcore porn clips on a site one of the boys had heard about from an older student.

Josiah, like his father and grandfather, had access to all sorts of unimaginable evil; yet he chose to turn his back on it and seek God's heart instead. Our boys too have access to all sorts of evil—much of it a few keystrokes away on a computer screen or gaming device. They too will have a choice: They can turn their backs on it to follow God, or they can conform to the times and follow the crowd. By setting a godly example, we can nudge them toward the right decision.

BRINGING IT home

Look up Romans 12:2. How can we avoid conforming to the world?

The Message states the passage this way: "Don't become so well-adjusted to your culture that you fit into it without even thinking. Instead, fix your attention on God. You'll be changed from the inside out."

What can you do to "fix your attention on God"?

How can you encourage your son to do the same?

In the process of helping your sons fix their attention on God, it will be essential to expose them to other godly male role models. As we progress through this study, consider godly men who might provide spiritual mentoring (either formally or by the example they set) for your sons.

Tomorrow we're going to dive in deeper and take a look at some specific godly character qualities Josiah possessed. As regents appointed to guide our sons in troubled times, our mission is to impart the same qualities to our boys so that they too might be renewed or "changed from the inside out."

INSTRUCTION MANUAL INCLUDED

let's talk **When my oldest son was about three, he received a train set from his grandparents. It was a sturdy, modern-day, plastic version of the train sets of days past. By the look on my boy's face, it was a home run. The train came complete with an elaborate track system and an instruction manual filled with a dozen "easy-to-assemble" track combinations—unless, of course, you happen to lose the instruction manual.**

"Your word is a lamp for my feet and a light on my path."
- Psalm 119:105

The manual went missing about two months after my son received it. Try as we might, we couldn't figure the thing out on our own.

Trust me, it would have been easier to figure out a Rubik's Cube® than the track combinations for this train set! After a few months of sitting in its original crazy eight pattern, the train found a new home on the top shelf of my son's closet—right next to a plastic bin of Lego® pieces that had once been part of a boxed Star Wars® set ... until the box with the picture of the fully assembled galaxy went MIA.

Such was a parent's plight in the pre-Internet, Google™-the-instruction-manual, good ole days.

GOD'S TAKE on the issue

Today we're going to talk about an instruction manual of far greater significance. The Book of the Law (either a copy of Deuteronomy or the Pentateuch, the first five books of the Old Testament) was viewed as God's instruction manual to the Jewish people. It detailed the creation account, the exodus from Egypt, and, more importantly, God's covenant with His children. The book went missing (or was destroyed) during the reigns of Manasseh or Amon. It comes as no surprise that it didn't seem to survive a line of self-serving kings who didn't want to answer to a holy God.

Fortunately, Josiah was a humble servant who desperately wanted to serve God. When the Book was discovered during the temple renovations he ordered, the king tore his robes and wept.

Read 2 Kings 23:1-24. What actions did Josiah take in the days that followed? (Check all that apply.)

_____ He read the Book of the Law to all the inhabitants of Jerusalem.

_____ He made a covenant to walk after the Lord and keep His commandments.

_____ He burned the vessels made for Baal and Asherah.

_____ He deposed the priests who had burned incense to Baal and other false gods.

_____ He broke down the houses of the male cult prostitutes.

_____ He broke down, burned, or defiled altars used for idol worship.

_____ He removed the bones from tombs of those who led Israel to sin, but spared the bones of the prophet who predicted Josiah's actions.

_____ He removed all the shrines of the high places built by the kings of Israel that provoked the Lord to anger.

_____ He sacrificed all the priests of the high places.

_____ He reinstated Passover, which had not been kept since the days of the judges.

Any one of the reforms would be noteworthy had it occurred as a solo act. But when you consider that King Josiah accomplished all of these reforms in spite of his dysfunctional family background, it makes it all the more awe-inspiring that this 26-year-old lad was able to rise above his circumstances to make a difference for God's glory.

We'll never know this side of eternity if Josiah's mother was truly linked to his unending devotion to God, but I can't help but picture her standing somewhere in the shadows with a knowing smile and a grateful heart.

> Read 2 Kings 23:25 to discover Josiah's legacy. Then fill in the blanks in the following legacy statement.
>
> If we are to raise godly sons, we must teach our sons to
> turn to the Lord with all their _____, all their
> _____, and all their _____.

What greater legacy can we hope for our sons than that they completely turn to God? But turning to the Lord proves impossible unless our sons possess two character qualities.

> Read 2 Kings 22:19. Which two key character qualities led to Josiah's sincere distress upon hearing the contents of the Book of the Law?
>
> 1.
>
> 2.

Depending on your Bible translation, the first quality was a tender or responsive heart over wrongdoing. I find it interesting that Josiah was sorrowful for sins he did not directly commit, accepting responsibility as a representative of the Israelite people who had strayed from God's commands.

To explain the young king's attitude, some translations use the word *penitent*, which in the original Hebrew means to "soften; (be, make) soft (-er), be tender."[5] Interestingly, our English word *penitentiary* derives from this term.

As we know, putting offenders in jail doesn't necessarily ensure that they will own their wrongful actions with a sincere and godly sorrow. Nor will sending our sons to time-out when they are toddlers, relegating them to their rooms when they are tweens, or grounding them for the weekend when they are teens. Directing our attention to the condition of their hearts must be part of the discipline process.

PERSONAL reflection

How might you encourage a penitent "softening of the heart" when your son does something wrong?

The second character quality leading to Josiah's sincere sorrow for wrongdoing was humility. If you look up the word *humble* in the dictionary, you'll find a definition much like this: "having or showing a low estimate of one's own importance."[6] The original Hebrew word for "humbled" in verse 19 is *kaw-nah´*, which means to "bend the knee; bring down (low), into subjection, under, humble (self), subdue."[7]

Josiah may have been king, but he knew he answered to a holy and perfect God. He possessed the rare quality of caring more about God's approval than the approval of men. Without the tenderness to God's laws and a humble recognition of the creative order—man answers to God—Josiah would have easily fallen into the same pattern of behavior as his father and grandfather.

Men like Josiah are not born; they're made. Yet without an awareness of sin and wrongdoing, a tender and humble response to sin is unlikely. Our sons are growing up in a culture in which the lines between right and wrong are blurred; it becomes easy to sin without second thought. As mothers, we must not hesitate to call attention to wrongdoing we witness in our sons' lives—not in an effort to beat them over the head and "guilt" them but rather to encourage them to respond in a manner pleasing to God.

BRINGING IT home

God has entrusted our sons to us; and they did, in fact, come with an instruction manual: the Bible. Yet in many homes, it's not uncommon for the instruction manual to sit on a bookshelf covered in a layer of dust. I doubt that's the case in your home, considering you are flipping through it to glean wisdom to complete this study, but does your boy know that the same instruction manual you've come to depend on is also his?

I recently came across this powerful statement during my morning devotion:

> "We can never really be exposed to the truths of God's Word without our lives being affected. Either we become more desirous of becoming like the author of the Book, or we become increasingly hardened to its truths. It has been said that we must know the Word of God in order to know the God of the Word."[8]

Reread that last quote. What does God's Word mean to you?

If we desire to become like the Author of the Book, we are more likely to raise sons who desire to become like the Author of the Book.

Real men know that in the journey called life, God's Word is their compass and God is their guide. What mother wouldn't love to hear her son declare as his life motto, "Your word is a lamp for my feet and a light on my path?" (Ps. 119:105).

WIRED FOR ADVENTURE

let's talk

If ever I needed proof that "adventure is written into the heart of a man," I'm fairly certain the homemade slip 'n' slide® my youngest son and his friends constructed could be submitted as evidence. They took up donations to purchase a roll of 40-by-100-foot plastic sheeting and 10 gallon-sized jugs of vegetable oil from the grocery store to turn their dream into a reality.

The boys rolled the plastic sheeting down a steep hill on the nearby campus of a middle school and *voila*, instant water park. That is, until the police showed up and kindly told them to slip 'n' slide on outta there.

I'm not sure if my son walked away from this adventure learning any lessons, but I certainly learned a few:

(1) Try as I might to temper my sons' testosterone, boys will still manage to be boys.

(2) No matter how many times you attempt to wash clothes soaked in vegetable oil, it will never come out. Forget about your boy ever wearing those clothes again.

> "Adventure is written into the heart of a man."[9]
> - John Eldredge

PERSONAL reflection

Share one (or more) of your son's memorable boyish adventures.

I doubt any mother of a son needs convincing that her son is wired for adventure from birth. As mothers we face the challenge of finding a reasonable balance when it comes to protecting our sons from danger without going overboard and inhibiting their God-given need for adventure. In the book *That's My Son*, author Rick Johnson notes: "Mothers, because of their nurturing tendencies, are often overprotective of their children. After all, it's a mother's job to civilize a boy."[10]

But boyish adventures provide a practice field for our sons to try out their budding manhood skills. (Yes, believe it or not, even homemade mega-sized slip 'n' slides can play a role in their manly development.) Many mothers, in their attempts to "civilize" their sons, thwart their attempts to become a man. John Eldredge notes that a boy's sense of adventure is not just about having fun. He expands the idea with, "Adventure requires something of us, puts us to the test. Though we may fear the test, at the same time we yearn to be tested, to discover that we have what it takes."[11]

Our female minds are incapable of fully understanding the effects of testosterone and the drive it produces in our sons to seek adventure. Our maternal impulses kick into high gear the moment our children enter the world; our highest goal is to protect them from harm.

Eldredge adds, "The recipe for fun is pretty simple raising boys: Add to any activity an element of danger, stir in a little exploration, add a dash of destruction, and you've got yourself a winner."[12] Just reading that sentence makes me sigh heavily. It certainly doesn't sound like a recipe for safety, now does it?

In our attempts to civilize our sons, we can discourage their appetites for adventure. I know I've been guilty, especially with my firstborn son. My goal was to keep him "safe" and out of the emergency room. Nothing is wrong with that goal unless you take it to the extreme and err on the side of opposing everything that poses a risk in their lives. Fortunately, God gave me a husband who insisted I loosen the reins.

Sometimes, I wonder how David's mother reacted when she found out he had killed Goliath with a slingshot. Had she seen him leave with his slingshot, would she have quizzed him with 20 questions on his way out the door?

What about John the Baptist's mother, Elizabeth? Did she try to send a care package of homemade goodies when she caught wind how he was living in the wilderness and dining on locusts and honey? And who can forget Mary, mother of Jesus? Was she ever tempted to put her boy on lockdown in an attempt to keep Him out of harm's way?

The women of ancient times were mothers just like we are and possessed the same nurturing and protective instincts to temper their sons' sense of adventure, but the Bible is full of stories of men who displayed amazing courage in exploits that would make most moms wince.

Following is a sampling of men whose adventures changed the course of history and are still recounted in Sunday School classes around the globe.

See if you can fill in the blanks without using the hints.

Noah and the _____ (Gen. 6:5-22)

Moses and the Ten _____ (Ex. 34:1-5)

David and _____ (1 Sam. 17:45-49)

Daniel and the _____ _____ (Dan. 6:1-28)

Jonah and the _____ (Jonah 1:1-17)

Now, I know what you're thinking: *C'mon, my son is not likely to face a nine-foot giant, be thrown into a lions' den, or be swallowed up by a big fish on the next family trip to the beach, so what's the point?* All of the men mentioned possessed a key ingredient that gave them the strength they needed: Courage.

Without courage King Josiah would never have initiated his lengthy reform campaign; instead, he would have become yet another male on his family tree who "did what was evil in the LORD's sight." Without courage David would have taken one look at the giant and run for the hills. Without courage Moses would have opted for a life better suited to a man accustomed to the comfort of the palace and many other perks afforded to him as the adopted son of the Pharaoh's daughter. Why take the risk of leading the Israelite people out of Egypt on a 40-year journey to the promised land?

Without courage, the disciples—many of whom died for the cause of Christ— would not have put their lives on the line so that the salvation message would reach the nations. Without courage Jesus would not have been obedient to death on a cross. Courage is a key ingredient in godly manhood.

Without courage and a practice field for it to blossom, our boys will remain boys. But we're not talking about just any old brand of courage. The courage exhibited by the men in the Bible was godly courage, bravery not based on reliance in their own strength but on an "I can do this with His help" attitude that was fueled by their faith in God and a dependence on Him to direct their steps.

One Scripture that I prayed often for my oldest son during his high-school years is 1 Corinthians 16:13-14: "Be on your guard; stand firm in the faith; be men of courage; be strong. Do everything in love" (NIV). The Greek word for the phrase "be men of courage" is *andrizomai*, which means "to act manly."[13] Interestingly, the ESV translates the passage this way: "Be watchful, stand firm in the faith, act like men, be strong."

Think about the phrase "act like men." How do you think God expects men to act?

What precedes the phrase in our passage?

Courage is more than the end result of a testosterone surge that prompts a brave act. Manly courage is godly courage, grounded in faith and seasoned with love.

CUTTING THE APRON STRINGS

let's talk **One of the greatest threats to a boy's budding manhood is the ever-present and overprotective "Helicopter Mom." Whether her mission is to bubble-wrap her son from a world of potential dangers or micro-manage his life down to the tiniest detail, her hovering tendencies can produce fallout for years to come.**

"When you are a mother, you are never really alone in your thoughts.

"A mother always has to think twice, once for herself and once for her child."[14]

- Sophia Loren

Consider this list of "hovering" behaviors to see whether you qualify as a Helicopter Mom. You might be a "Helicopter Mom" if you (check all that apply):

____ Repeatedly deliver your child's lunch/backpack/gym clothes to the school when he leaves it behind

____ Hesitate to take the training wheels off your child's bike when he is entering middle school

____ Manage your middle/high-schooler's day-timer and keep track of his assignment/test due dates (Bonus points if you know the last three test grades.)

____ Require your child to carry hand sanitizer and lather up before/after every meal/snack and bathe in it after playing outside

_____ Actually followed the recommended protocol of sterilizing pacifiers/
toys/bottle nipples (You get a free pass if it was your first child.)

_____ Find yourself saying things like: "We're registered to take the
SAT this Saturday" or "We're going to play coach-pitch baseball
next year instead of tee-ball" (Key word: "we")

_____ Ever stayed up late working on a class project after your child has
gone to bed so he does not face a late penalty

_____ Ever signed your child up for more than two extracurricular
activities in one season (And two can be excessive, depending on
the type of activity and time required.)

_____ Contacted your child's teacher/coach to argue an injustice (such
as not enough playing time) rather than requiring your child to
address the problem on his own (if a true injustice has occurred)

It's a mother's nature to protect her children from the dangers of the world and look for ways to help them get ahead. However, if we're not careful we can go overboard with our hovering tendencies and provoke (or exasperate or embitter or aggravate) our children to anger (Col. 3:21). The key is to find a healthy balance by being a "protector" without becoming a "provoker."

PERSONAL reflection

Consider recent interactions with your son. Based on his response
to you, how does he interpret your behavior?

● Protective   ● Somewhere in the middle
● Provoking   ● I'm not sure

Some mothers have a tendency to overprotect their children because they are seeking control over dangers, both real and perceived, that threaten to harm their children. Others obsess over their children's academic progress in order to control their destinies and provide them with future happiness. Still other mothers may hover when it comes to image-maintenance issues such as staying in shape, dressing attractively, wearing name brands, or owning the latest gadgets.

But while at first glance hovering Helicopter Moms may appear to have their child's best interests in mind, their high need for control is unhealthily rooted in fear. Fear of danger. Fear their child will not find future success (as defined by Helicopter Mom). Fear their children may not be accepted if they don't look or perform a certain way. In a nutshell, Helicopter Moms want to ensure that their children turn out according to their personal script and time line.

If you worry that you may qualify as a Helicopter Mom, you're not alone. Numerous biblical accounts highlight doting, overbearing mothers whose attempts to control their sons' futures produced some fallout that can surely teach us.

GOD'S TAKE on the issue

Read Matthew 20:20-24. What did the mother of the sons of Zebedee ask of Jesus?

And you thought coaches had it rough dealing with pesky mothers! I find it interesting that in spite of the fact that the boys' mother asked the favor, Jesus directed His answer to the boys and made no acknowledgment of their mother. By ignoring her, He conveyed, "C'mon, guys. Let's take Mama out of the middle and talk this out man-to-man."

What do you suppose was the mother's goal in wanting her sons to sit at the right and left hand of Jesus?

_____ Special favor, what else could it be? She wanted to brag in her annual Christmas letter.

_____ It's all about networking. She was hoping her boys could hook her up someday with a mansion in the Pearly Gates Estates.

_____ "You have not because you ask not." Sitting on the bench in this game is not an option.

_____ A little bit of all of the above.

PERSONAL reflection

Describe a time when you went to bat for your son in order to gain preferential treatment.

Our tendency is to justify that our "meddling" is the only way to gain fair treatment for our sons.

Reflect on Matthew 20:24. How did Mrs. Zebedee's attempt to secure a favorable outcome for her sons end up working against them?

How do you think her actions impacted her relationship with her sons?

BRINGING IT home

In order for our sons to develop a healthy masculinity, we must resist the urge to fight their battles for them. (And all the teachers and coaches yelled, "Amen!")

Read the following three scenarios, and write alternative solutions that help empower our sons to fight their own battles.

1. Your son is on a basketball team, but he spends most of his time warming the bench. Last season he played for a different team and was one of the leading scorers, but his current coach has yet to give him a chance to prove himself. You decide to take matters into your own hands and give the coach a call.

Alternative solution:

2. You are checking your son's mid-term grade report and notice that he has a missing assignment in one class that will make a huge impact on his grade average. You ask your son about it, and he insists he turned it in. You make a note on your calendar to call his teacher the next day and resolve the matter.

Alternative solution:

3. Your teenage son needs a summer job, but he lacks initiative when it comes to a job search. You receive a job lead from a business owner in your church who sent out an e-mail looking for students in need of summer work. You don't want the opportunity to fall through the cracks so you immediately reply to the e-mail, touting your son's experience and availability.

Alternative solution:

While some circumstances may merit a mom intervention, they should be the exception, not the rule. While it can be painful to stand by and watch our sons suffer an injustice such as not getting enough playing time in a sport, failing to win a much-deserved award, or not getting the preferred homeroom teacher, the truth is, life is not always fair. It is far more valuable for our sons to learn to depend on God when life is unfair than to depend on Mom to come to the rescue.

GOD'S TAKE on the issue

When it comes to moms who stop at nothing for achieving a desired outcome for their sons, Jacob's mother, Rebekah, tops the list. Here's a quick synopsis of one dysfunctional family situation.

In Genesis 27 Rebekah, mother of grown twins Jacob and Esau, decided that without her intervention, her favorite child would miss out. As her near-blind husband, Isaac, prepared to pass on the promised blessing—the rights generally granted by the patriarch to rule the clan—to elder son Esau, Rebekah insisted that Jacob pose as his older brother and take what his father planned to give. Rebekah's deceptive plan worked, and Jacob received his father's blessing (27:1-29).

While Rebekah's actions may seem unspeakable, in her defense, God's sovereign will was being played out. Let's look back at some early family records to see how.

Summarize Genesis 25:19-23 here.

Read Genesis 25:24-28. Whom did Isaac love and why?
Whom did Rebekah love and why? (See v. 27 for a hint.)

Jacob was a homebody or, as some might conclude, a bit of a "mama's boy." Esau, on the other hand, was interested in more manly pursuits. He may not have given Mom much thought. Appreciation, after all, wasn't one of his strong points.

Read Genesis 25:29-34. How important was the birthright to Esau?

The family birthright consisted of special privileges, again typically for the first-born male. Chief among those privileges was a double portion of the family estate as an inheritance.

If you have a teenage son in your home who spends half his day staring into the pantry mumbling, "I'm staaarving," chances are you understand Esau's exaggerative declaration that he was "about to die" of hunger. I can't imagine there wasn't something in the tent to satisfy Esau's growling stomach. We aren't told this detail, but I wouldn't be surprised if Rebekah hadn't mentioned God's providence at some point within the hearing distance of her boys. It would certainly explain Esau's disinterest in the birthright.

While Rebekah's trickery related to the blessing (Gen. 27) fulfilled the providence of God's plan that "the older will serve the younger" (Gen. 25:23), the means of obtaining the blessing is hard to justify given God's character. God is God, and He can accomplish His divine purposes however He chooses; yet this in no way suggests God would approve of Rebekah's sin.

Read Genesis 27:41-45.

Any excitement over Jacob being awarded the blessing was short-lived as his brother plotted to kill him. To save her son's life, Rebekah sent him to another country to find a wife among her relatives. Surely she didn't think that her son would be gone for two decades. I imagine that during those years Rebekah tormented herself by rehashing the details of the trickery used to gain the blessing. I can't help but think she came to the conclusion that relying on God's script and timing would have been a much better plan.

Twenty years later Jacob returned to his homeland. Esau's heart had finally softened, and when he heard Jacob was coming home, he set out to meet him (Gen. 33:1-4). It was a sweet reunion, but the story ends with no mention of their mother. Many theologians believe Rebekah died during his absence.

What consequences do you think Rebekah's actions caused Jacob?

Esau?

Isaac?

Rebekah did not need to take matters into her own hands to fulfill God's divine will.

What might mothers today learn from Rebekah's story?

As mothers, we are to raise our sons to be the men God created them to be—not the men we may want them to be. God wired them for adventure, and it is not our job to civilize or manipulate our sons. Instead, we want to help them understand God's definition of true manhood, teaching them to pursue His ways.

WRAPPING IT up

In C. S. Lewis's essay *The Necessity of Chivalry*, he wrote that "the disparate strands of manhood—fierceness and gentleness—can find healthy synthesis in the person of the knight and in the code of chivalry. Here these competing impulses—normally found in different individuals—find their union."[15] "Testosterone-fueled" manliness that is not tempered with compassion and tenderness can result in too much brute and not enough heart. Both qualities must be in submission to God.

I want to end by reflecting on powerful statements on the life of King Josiah:

> "We sow in youth what we reap in young manhood; as we go on our way we gather in the harvest of the thought and toil of the years that came before it. But this applies to our moral and spiritual character more perfectly than to anything else. How, then, can we afford to lose the great advantage of building up from the beginning? Our manhood will be much the weaker for an ill-spent youth, and much the stronger for a well-spent one. Our whole life will be greatly impoverished by the one, greatly enriched by the other."[16]

As I read these statements, it struck me that a mother's role is to provide her son with "the great advantage of building up from the beginning."[17] Allow me to brag on you for a minute as we close: By committing to this study, you are taking a step to fulfill that role! Close by praying about the truths He has taught you this week.

CONVERSATION 2

"What you don't learn to conquer may become your master."

Helpful verses on self-control: 1 Corinthians 10:13;
1 Corinthians 6:12; 2 Peter 2:19; Romans 6:16

Enslaved: "cause to _____ _____ _____

_____ _____ _____; make subject to a habit."

Solution: A good formula is STP (STOP, THINK, PRAY)
_____: Stop. Regroup. Replace.
Take _____every thought (2 Cor. 10:5).

We must _____ _____ _____ _____ _____ to
replace tempting thoughts or activities with wholesome ones.

_____: If you've ever wondered about your sons, What *were
they thinking?*, they weren't! The frontal lobe is that center of the brain
that _____ _____ to decisions and actions.

_____: The most powerful thing they can do is _____ _____

_____ _____ _____ _____ _____ to
resist temptations (Matt. 26:41).

CONVERSATION STARTERS with your group:

What most concerns you about what your sons will face?
What most encourages you?

Leslie shared how Son Time every night throughout their lives yields
special benefits for her family. Share similar experiences you have had
with your sons. Or what could you start doing right now?

*Interested in reviewing this or other 5 Conversations Bible study sessions?
You can download all digital sessions by going to www.lifeway.com/women*

WEEK 2

Choosing Sides

Alfred
Lord
Tennyson

~

"The happiness of a man in this life does not consist in the absence but in the mastery of his passion."[1]

THE ANATOMY OF A DOWNFALL

let's talk **Over coffee a friend opened up about a struggle she was experiencing in her marriage. In a voice raw with pain she struggled to speak: "My husband is ... a sex addict."**

I responded with words of sorrow and tender compassion; but given the times, I can't say I was surprised by the disclosure.

If you think you know the profile of a sex addict, think again. My friend—a beautiful, young mother of three—shared that her husband is a family man who was raised in the church and even taught Sunday School for many years. But he kept a secret—a deep, dark secret exposed only when his wife received his shocking phone call in the middle of the night.

He was supposed to be out of town on a business trip hundreds of miles from home; instead, he had been arrested locally for soliciting a prostitute. He needed his wife to contact an attorney.

The conversation seemed so far-fetched that she reasoned he was playing a practical joke. Only when he began to softly cry over the phone and repeatedly mumble "I'm so, so sorry," did she realize he was serious.

In the weeks that followed, the husband came clean about his double life, including his interest in hardcore porn, time spent with paid escorts, and his occasional visits

"There is a charm about the forbidden that makes it unspeakably desirable."[2]

- Mark Twain

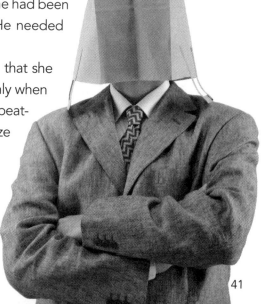

41

to strip clubs. While the couple has taken steps to repair the damage caused by his choices, they know a long road of healing lies ahead.

How does something like this happen? My friend offered a clue when she shared a disclosure her husband made in a subsequent counseling session: He began viewing porn in his high-school years, and it developed into a habit he couldn't shake.

A downfall doesn't become a downfall the moment someone gets caught; instead, it begins when a sin gains a position of control in the heart and mind. The downfall of my friend's husband, for example, began when he started viewing porn and then cultivated the habit by returning to his sin. As in his case, many downfalls find their point of origin (that stand-at-the-crossroads-moment) back in middle school, high school, or college.

While we cannot control the choices our sons will make when standing at a tempting crossroad, we can educate them about the fallout that can result from allowing sin to master them. More importantly, we can make them aware of the sequence of events that often precedes a downfall, in hopes that they might recognize the trap before it snaps and takes them captive.

List 3-5 common sins that threaten to master our sons.

Enslavement to sin always produces collateral damage. Just ask Tammy, who responded to a survey question I posted on my blog. When I asked my reader-moms to share their most pressing concerns in raising their sons, she replied this way:

> One day my husband of 15 years, with a 9-year-old daughter and a 6-year-old son, decided he was going to abandon his family and marry another woman, 13 years younger. Within 9 months of his leaving, he had his vasectomy reversed and remarried. In their first year of marriage he had another child—a boy. He has had little to no interaction with our children in over four years.
>
> How do I teach our son to be morally sound when he has been exposed to such blatant infidelity. Help!

Many mothers like Tammy carry a heavy burden when it comes to raising their sons to be godly men. If you face a similar challenge, please don't grow discouraged or give up hope. Your efforts will make a difference. By exposing your son to God's truths, he will better recognize that true freedom and happiness are found only in Christ.

 PERSONAL reflection

Describe a personal situation that involved enslavement to a sin and resulted in collateral damage.

At what point did the downfall begin?

What preventative steps might have been taken to avoid it?

GOD'S TAKE on the issue

When it comes to downfalls, the Bible is full of cautionary examples. From Adam and Eve's decision to eat the one fruit forbidden them to Judas's betrayal of Jesus, we find no shortage of examples to share with our boys.

Let's focus on the life story of King David, a highly respected and courageous man who chose to walk headfirst into a mess.

Read 2 Samuel 11.

Talk about a story ripe for the cover of *National Enquirer*! David, the humble shepherd boy handpicked by God for Israel's throne, took a fall—and a BIG one at that. This same magnificent man rose to early fame when he slew Goliath, the giant. And frankly, his courageous acts of obedience to God in the years before his downfall prove far too numerous to list.

One Bible commentary sheds light on the season of David's life when his crossroads moment occurred:

> "He was about fifty years of age; had been reigning in Jerusalem upwards of twelve years; dwelt in a stately palace on Mount Zion; and possessed numerous sons and daughters, a splendid court and a powerful army. He had been 'preserved whithersoever he went,' subdued his enemies, and returned in triumph. His natural gifts and fervent piety were even more extraordinary than his material prosperity; and he now stood on the pinnacle of human greatness and glory."[3]

Yet David—blessed and at the peak of his game—proves that no one is exempt from a downfall. An old expression warns, "We are all just one step shy of tomorrow's headlines." David (aka: "a man after God's own heart") reminds us that even God's most devoted warriors have chinks in their armor.

Which of the following best describes David's "chink"?
● Greed ● Lust ● Dislike for Uriah ● Selfishness

In 2 Samuel 11 David made three attempts to cover up his sin with Bathsheba.

Complete the sentences to summarize his actions.
1. In verse 8, David ...

2. In verse 13, he ...

3. In verses 14-15, he ...

What was Uriah's excuse for not going home to eat and sleep with his wife (v. 11)?

Uriah's humble explanation did nothing to trigger awareness in David that he was in a downward spiral. In fact, Uriah's noble explanation and David's subsequent decision to have him moved to the front line and essentially murdered speaks volumes about the power of sin in David's life. This brings up an important question: Which was in the position of control—David or his sin of lust?

Don't be fooled. A sin's mastery always produces misery. The first few stops on the road to mastery may be pleasurable and fun, but sin has a way of eventually taking captives and robbing victims of their freedom. I imagine David had a rather good time acting out his desire to bed Bathsheba. But when weeks later Bathsheba sent word to David that she was expecting his love child, the fallout began.

It's important we not gloss over the account of David's sin. Within 2 Samuel 11 we find enough drama and dysfunction to inspire a "48 Hours" murder mystery or maybe even a reality series based on the Real Housewives of King David. One can only imagine the sordid details and roller coaster of emotions represented by this story. Consider Bathsheba's certain panic when she missed her period—or her worry over a possible death sentence (stoning was a customary punishment for adultery).

Imagine the sleepless nights David experienced as he rehearsed possible strategies to cover up his actions. And these represent only the beginning of the collateral damage that occurred as the result of David's indulgence with Bathsheba. The painful consequences were far-reaching and plagued the king's home for many years to come.

BRINGING IT home

David's downfall serves as a reminder to teach our sons the discipline of self-control. It's no accident that Galatians 5:22-23 mentions self-control as a fruit of the Spirit. Our sons are not born with a natural desire for self-control; therefore, it is up to us to teach them its importance. This discipline proves necessary to win mastery over sin and temptations.

How might self-control help your son overcome:
Sexual temptation?

Lying?

Disobedience?

Vocal outbursts?

Parents can modify behavior to a limited degree, but the "self" portion of self-control leaves the ultimate decision up to our children. Without this learned ability to control impulses, however, our sons will tend to pursue every gluttonous pleasure that crosses their paths. So while they are under our umbrella of care, we can attempt to block their pursuit of unwholesome pleasures, knowing that in the end they will need to practice self-control as a primary line of defense.

The next time we're together we'll pick back up with David's story and take a more detailed look at his progression into sin. More importantly, we will discuss practical ways to teach our sons self-control.

AS A MAN THINKS IN HIS HEART

let's talk **Unwholesome desires occasionally knock on the doors of all hearts. The real danger comes when we invite them to come in, grab a seat, and stay a while. David didn't cave to sin in one moment of weakness. A sequence of events led to David's downfall.**

"If passion drives you, let reason hold the reins."[4]

- Benjamin Franklin

In order to better understand what our sons may face as well as the slow and steady progression of sin, I want to dissect the four verses that changed the course of King David's life.

Correctly number the sequence of events that occur in 2 Samuel 11:2-4.

____ The king sleeps with Bathsheba.

____ David takes an evening stroll on the roof.

____ The king sends messengers to bring the woman to him.

____ David asks about the woman he sees, learning that she is married.

Read James 1:13-15, and write out verse 15.

God does not hold responsibility for the temptations that come our way. Instead, we experience temptation when our own evil desires begin to tug at our hearts and toy with our minds.

At what point did David's desire for Bathsheba enter the picture?

_____ When he rose from the couch after a mid-day nap

_____ When she showed up at the palace door wearing a low-cut tunic and selling magazine subscriptions

_____ When he walked along the roof of his house and spotted Bathsheba bathing

_____ When he sent for her and she came to the palace

At what point did his desire give birth to sin?

_____ When he inquired about the woman

_____ When he sent for her anyway in spite of being told she was another man's wife

_____ When he slept with her

_____ When he failed to use protection and she became pregnant as a result

One Bible commentary notes, "When once the rein is given to such passions, the fall has taken place in essence. When David saw and looked on her, with a certain thought in his mind and feeling in his heart, he had virtually done the deed of which we have a record. In the spiritual sphere, thought and desire are tantamount to deed. The one is but the fuller form of the other. Sin lies in intent and purpose, whether it be actualized in outward fact or not."[5]

While some may argue that David should have avoided the rooftop in the first place, keep in mind that he did not go looking for sin. Nothing in the passage indicates that David was in the habit of taking walks on his rooftop to indulge in Peeping Tom fantasies. According to one commentary: "It was usual in Palestine, and remains so in all hot countries, to take a siesta in the heat of the day; and, on awaking, David walked backward and forward on the flat roof of his house, to enjoy the cool breezes of the evening. In so doing he was probably following his usual habits; but temptation came upon him, as so often is the case, unexpectedly."[6]

> List unwholesome desires your son might experience that could give birth to sin. (Note: If your son is old enough to swipe another child's toy in the church preschool, this question is for you too!)

As is often the scenario with sin, David was caught off guard and in a split second was faced with a choice. Unfortunately, he made the wrong decision and followed it with several more. But momentary desire does not always result in sin. And while everyone will experience unwholesome desires, not everyone will entertain them.

Just as importantly, as one commentary notes, "Though God may suffer his people to fall into sin; he will not suffer them to lie still in it."[7] Should David have been given the opportunity for a do-over, I imagine he would have skipped the rooftop walk altogether or, at the very least, prohibited his eyes from wandering.

> Wandering eyes draw our sons to sin too. Read Job 31:1.
> What did Job do to solve the problem of wandering eyes?

In my book *Your Boy*, I discuss how my husband and I taught our sons the principle of "bouncing their eyes," a concept introduced in Steve Arterburn's *Every Young Man's Battle*. The idea is that in an attempt to shield themselves from the constant barrage of inappropriate images or for that matter, the scantily clad women that cross their paths, young men should immediately avert their gazes when they see something that causes their thoughts to wander. Imagine the heartache that could have been avoided had David simply bounced his eyes when Bathsheba showed up in his line of vision!

To expect our sons never to have an unwholesome thought or desire is unreasonable and sets them up for failure. When even we can't claim success, how can we expect them to never have an impure thought? The key to whether or not a desire gives birth to sin lies in the steps that follow the initial desire. What do we do in that moment when we first face temptation?

Imagine that your son stands in David's sandals and is about to head up on that roof for a walk. If you knew he was about to catch a glimpse of a bathing beauty, what conversation would you want to have to stop desire from progressing to sin?

CONVERSATION boosters

Let's try something more practical. Consider the following real-life scenarios submitted to my blog. After reading each one, jot down the actions you would take, as well as the conversation you would have with your son if he were involved in the same situation.

1. Cheryl's issue: Video games/boundaries

My son is 11. I'm concerned about his addiction to video games. We have limited his use of games to the weekends (assuming he meets certain benchmarks), and I have noticed he does much better in attitude and openness to spiritual things when he's not allowed to play. However, when he spends time with his friends, that's exactly what they want to do: play video games. I know he is young, but I want him to be able to set his own boundaries.

Actions you would take:

Your conversation:

2. Pam's issue: Cell phone texting/language

My youngest son is 14, a freshman in high school. Last spring I caught him texting a girl a year younger. It was bad enough that he was disobeying us by using his phone after bedtime, but when I saw what he had texted I was shocked. His message was full of sexual innuendo and obscenities!

My child is a believer, is being raised in a solid Christian home, and has been taught the Bible since birth. In addition, my husband and I are leaders in the church. We do not use such language and do not allow filth into our home. Our son does not have a computer or TV in his room (those are filtered and located where we can monitor his viewing), and he is hardly ever left alone in the house. I was shocked and so terribly disappointed in him.

Actions you would take:

Your conversation:

3. Amy's issue: Impulsive behavior at a very early age

I have a five-year-old son, our only child. I've noticed that he's incredibly impulsive (more so, it seems, than his friends). This worries me about what may come down the pipe in the future. He recently took a toy from a friend's house. When I asked him why he stole the toy, he replied, "Because I wanted it."

Actions you would take:

Your conversation:

I know it's hard to think through these scenarios, especially if you have a little one and weren't aware of the challenges that may lie ahead! But I want to encourage you to hone your skills in developing and engaging in key conversations with your sons. Hopefully, your conversations can touch on self-control and the long-term consequences that occur if desire gives birth to sin and sin, in turn, gains a level of mastery.

David's sin would follow him for the remainder of his life, proving that enslavement to sin always comes with a price. As mothers, we owe our sons full disclosure regarding the dangers associated with a lack of self-control.

IGNORANCE IS NOT BLISS

let's talk **If I had to sum up David's downfall in one sentence, it would boil down to this: David chose to indulge the sinful desires of his flesh rather than live by the Spirit. And we'd all be lying if we didn't admit that we too at times tend to indulge in sinful desires rather than live the way God desires, by the Spirit. Our sons are the same way.**

"Do not bite at the bait of pleasure, till you know there is no hook beneath it."[8]

- Thomas Jefferson

Sin is not a behavior; it is a condition based on a nature that turns away from God. A particular sin for one person may not reach a level of mastery, but for another, it could prove a lifelong snare.

Not every boy who sees porn will become a sex addict. Not every boy who experiments with alcohol will become an alcoholic. Not every boy who smokes pot will become a pothead. Not every boy who plays nonstop video games will grow up into a lazy bum. While the behavior violates God's standard for everyone who engages in it, some young men will find themselves more predisposed than others to enslavement by certain sins.

That's why we must draw boundaries in an effort to safeguard them. In the end, however, our sons will choose how to live their lives.

Read Galatians 5:16-18. In what two ways can we live?

1.

2.

The King James Version uses the phrase "lust of the flesh" to better identify Paul's point. The Greek word for lust is *epithumia*, which means "a longing (especially for what is forbidden)."[9]

Living by the Spirit and living for the flesh are at odds with one another. As we long for the forbidden, we fail to long for God. It's hard, then, to live a duplicitous life without it taking a heavy toll on the soul. At some point, we must choose.

Living by the Spirit doesn't mean we won't sin. It simply means we are set free and don't have to give into the craving for sin. The person who chooses to live by the Spirit yet falls into sin (which will happen from time to time) is miserable, because sin is at odds with the Spirit that lives within her.

Read Galatians 5:19-23, and fill in the chart.

Works of the Flesh	Fruit of the Spirit

Circle the spiritual fruit that proves most helpful in avoiding the works of the flesh.

The Greek word for self-control is *egkrateia*, which can be defined as the "virtue of one who masters his desires and passions, especially his sensual appetites."[10] Can you imagine the heartache that could be avoided if our sons learned to master their "desires and passions"? Self-control is arguably a godly discipline mastered only by the indwelling of the Holy Spirit.

Read 2 Peter 1:4-8, and write verse 6 here. (Also re-read v. 5.)
Underline the factor that leads to self-control.

Self-control is a by-product of knowing God. If we want to raise self-controlled sons, we must first introduce them to God and the beauty of the gospel. This doesn't mean we drop them off at church each Sunday and trust that, by default of being there, they will develop a thriving relationship with Christ.

Regular church attendance is only part of the equation. God has appointed parents as the primary disciplers of our sons. As a result, more may be caught than taught during the years our sons spend with us.

PERSONAL reflection

What positive moral lesson were you "taught" as a child?

What wisdom did you "catch" as a result of watching the example of someone's life?

Our priority should not be to simply teach our sons self-control but first and foremost to reveal to them the grace of God. In other words, we are to live out the beauty of the gospel in front of our children. Titus 2:11-14 sums it up well:

> "For the grace of God has appeared with salvation for all people, instructing us to deny godlessness and worldly lusts and to live in a sensible, righteous, and godly way in the present age, while we wait for the blessed hope and appearing of the glory of our great God and Savior, Jesus Christ. He gave Himself for us to redeem us from all lawlessness and to cleanse for Himself a people for His own possession, eager to do good works."

Attempting to teach our sons self-control apart from the power of Christ is futile. In fact, it's not only futile, it's also dangerous. Jesus directed some of His harshest criticism at the Pharisees and their focus on "behavior modification" rather than "heart inhabitation."

We all have a gluttonous, self-seeking desire to hop from one pleasure to another. Yet chasing after these desires leaves us empty in the end. Helping our sons understand this paradox creates a beautiful opportunity to introduce the gospel of Christ and to show them their obvious need for a Savior.

Read Galatians 5:24-25. Who is able to crucify (or kill) the sinful nature?

I love Paul's final charge at the end of this passage: "Since we live by the Spirit, let us keep in step with the Spirit" (NIV). As parents, we have a responsibility to help our children "keep in step" by raising them in a Spirit-filled environment and exposing them to Spirit-filled activities. Part of that responsibility includes monitoring their peer groups and nudging them toward the kind of friends who will help, rather than hinder, their ability to keep in step with the Spirit.

Benjamin Franklin once said, "He that lies down with the dogs, shall rise up with fleas."[11] If you've ever had to treat a flea-infested dog, you would agree that it's far better to take preventative measures on the front end than to tackle the problem after the fact.

Write 1 Corinthians 15:33 here.

Describe a situation that illustrates the truth of this verse. It's OK to use an example from the media.

In helping our kids choose positive peer groups, we explained to them the difference between "weekday friends" and "weekend friends." A "weekday friend" might be one my son meets at school or in an after-school activity: Their friendship is primarily built during school hours or during the time spent in a common activity. Any time spent together after school or on weekends would be at our home in a monitored setting. A "weekend friend" might be someone with similar beliefs and values as my son. I would not hesitate to have this child over on the weekends or to allow my son to spend time with the friend away from our house. Obviously, the "weekend friend" list is much shorter list than the "weekday friend" list.

Teaching our children this distinction gave us a baseline for helping them choose a positive, "parent-approved" peer group. For example, if my son expressed a desire to get together with a "weekday friend" from school, we had the condition that the friend would come to our house until we could get to know him and develop a better feel for the situation. This friend may or may not transition into a "weekend friend." In some situations, our sons had friends they strictly saw at our home because we did not have an adequate comfort level in allowing our sons to spend time at the friend's house.

Rate the importance you place on monitoring your son's peer group.
● High ● Moderate ● Low

Describe a situation in which peer group influenced your child's behavior, whether for good or bad.

Few will choose to live for the Spirit, and you won't find anyone out there who has a perfect track record in doing so. But there are those who are trying, even though they may have some slip-ups along the way. If your son is a believer and truly desires to live by the Spirit rather than indulge the passions and desires of his flesh, he will gravitate toward those who hold similar values and beliefs.

As mothers, we are wise to closely monitor our sons' peer groups and draw some boundaries when necessary. Proverbs chapter 1 offers valuable wisdom when it comes to choosing friends: "My son, if sinners entice you, do not give in to them … my son, do not go along with them, do not set foot on their paths; for their feet rush into sin" (Prov. 1:10,15-16, NIV). Until our sons have the wisdom and discernment to keep a distance from those who might "entice" or tempt them to "rush into sin," it's up to us to help them keep a distance.

HEART OF THE MATTER

let's talk **Regardless of the measures we take to expose our sons to godly influences, we cannot make them live by the Spirit. We can set up tight boundaries in an attempt to discourage ungodly choices, but alas, we cannot change their hearts. In fact, we can't even ensure that they are Spirit-filled.**

It is quite possible for a child to grow up in a Christian home and attend church on a regular basis and still not know Christ. Even those who correctly identify themselves as Christians are quite simply "Christ followers"—sinners saved by grace. While not perfect, they strive to live their lives in accordance with God's good and pleasing will.

Sometimes our sons will fall into temptation because "the spirit is willing, but the flesh is weak" (Matt. 26:41). Like us, our sons will occasionally stand at the crossroads of temptation and take a wrong turn. Slip-ups are inevitable, but when a believer slips up, he or she reacts differently to sin. When Christ followers take a wrong turn, God, in His loving patience, places U-turn signs along the way, encouraging us to turn back.

God's U-turn sign for King David arrived with an unexpected visit from the prophet Nathan.

"Of all acts of man repentance is the most divine. The greatest of all faults is to be conscious of none."[12]

– Thomas Carlyle

GOD'S TAKE on the issue

Read 2 Samuel 12:1-13. According to verse 1, how did the meeting between Nathan and David come about?

Why do you think God sent Nathan to confront David about his sin?

_____ God wanted to trap David and exercise stern judgment and wrath on him.

_____ God wanted to convict David over his sin in order that he might be restored in his relationship with God.

_____ God wanted people to realize that David's story had all the makings of a reality show script, so He sent along a crew with hidden cameras to catch his reaction.

On arrival, Nathan told David a story about a man whose precious lamb was taken by a wealthy traveling stranger who had no shortage of sheep in his own flock.

Match each character in the story with the real-life person it represents.

_____ Sheep owner   a. David

_____ Traveling stranger   b. Bathsheba

_____ Lamb   c. Uriah

Summarize David's initial response to the story (vv. 5-6).

See verse 7. What does Nathan say in response to David's anger over the selfishness of the "traveling stranger"?

_____ are the man!

PERSONAL reflection

Describe a situation when someone acted as a "Nathan" in your life. How did you respond?

What question did Nathan ask David in verse 9?

In spite of David's attempts to cover up his sin, he couldn't hide the truth from God. There is no such thing as secret sin. As parents, we need to remind our children of this truth. While we prefer that our sons respond to conviction at the Spirit's initial prompting, sometimes confrontation or even a tough-love approach proves necessary to getting them back on track.

In other words, God often calls parents to act as Nathans in their children's lives. If we are aware of a sin, we do our sons an injustice to ignore it.

How common do you think it is today for parents to call attention to the sin in their children's lives?

● Very   ● Somewhat   ● Highly Unlikely

Explain how ignoring a child's sin does him an injustice.

How did David respond to the news of what would happen as a result of his sin with Bathsheba (v. 13)?

When someone is caught in a sin and confronted, he or she has two choices: to repent of it or to refuse to recognize the actions as wrong. One Bible commentary notes, "The first step of the impenitent sinner is to cling to his sin."[13]

PERSONAL reflection

Describe a situation in which you (or someone close to you) lacked repentance, opting instead to cling to sin. What happened as a result of that choice?

Did David cling to his sin?

   ● Yes   ● No   ● I'm not sure

Read Psalm 51:1-17, which David wrote in response to his sin with Bathsheba. Now read 2 Corinthians 7:10. What two types of sorrow does the verse mention?

Consider what you know of David's response to God's discipline. What indicates that his sorrow was godly and not worldly?

In acknowledging that he had rebelled against the Lord, David expressed godly sorrow; but he still paid a heavy price for his actions. One commentary writer notes, "David's sin was heinous, but the grace of God was more than sufficient to forgive and restore him. … And yet, though David could be restored to fellowship with his God, the impact of his sin remained and would continue to work its sorrow in the nation as well as in the king's life."[14]

As part of his sentence for the sin, David lost the child born to Bathsheba. He endured years of turmoil within his own house that included the rape of one of his daughters (by her half brother, Amnon), the avenging murder of Amnon by another son, and David's humiliation when his son Absalom slept with some of David's wives and concubines, publicly disgracing him.

But one of David's greatest heartaches came when Absalom attempted to seize the throne from his father, once again putting David on the run to escape death. Absalom was eventually killed, but David—even though betrayed by Absalom— still mourned his son's death.

BRINGING IT home

The pursuit of a few pleasurable moments can lead to a lifetime of painful consequences. In spite of David's sin and the resulting fallout, God called David a man after His own heart. While it's easy to assume this conclusion was based on David's life prior to his sin, God is sovereign and knew the details of the time line representing David's life in advance: the good, the bad, and the ugly. What hope this offers us all!

Living as a man after God's own heart does not require that our sons achieve perfection. But it does require that their hearts grow sensitive and malleable to God's leading, even in response to conviction over sin.

While in the process of writing the book version of this study, I had to act as a Nathan in my youngest son's life. (Lovely timing, wouldn't you say?) While spot-checking his phone one afternoon, I read several text messages indicating he was engaged in a sinful behavior. Honestly, it would have been easier for me to ignore the evidence and pray for my boy from the sidelines.

While it's almost always difficult to confront sin, I knew God had allowed me to see those text messages for a reason. When my husband and I sat our boy down for a heart-to-heart discussion, he came clean, even expressing relief over getting caught. Tears fell as he expressed sincere, godly sorrow—a major indicator in assessing the condition of his heart.

Interestingly, several other young men were involved in the sinful behavior; as a result I notified their parents. All of the young men involved in the situation profess to be believers, and they all expressed remorse when confronted by their parents. My son made the observation months later, however, that while they all sounded sorry, a handful expressed only a worldly sorrow over having been caught. If their sorrow is rooted in anything less than honest repentance, chances are they will eventually return to the sinful behavior once the pain of the consequences wears off. True mastery over sin can only occur with a godly sorrow that leads to hear change. Repentance brings freedom.

We will make mistakes, but God offers love, grace, and mercy in spite of them. He is in the business of restoring lives by providing the sinner with something he can't obtain for himself: forgiveness. Only in recognizing this amazing truth are we able to respond to the sin in our lives with sincere, godly sorrow.

Romans 5:8 reminds us: "But God proves His own love for us in that while we were still sinners, Christ died for us!" That also means that "while our sons were still sinners, Christ died for them" as well.

A NEVER-ENDING BATTLE

let's talk **As we wrap up our discussion on principles to help our sons gain mastery over sin, I want to end with a timely reminder: The struggle with sin is ongoing. We can attest to the validity of that statement based on our personal struggles with sin, but is it possible we sometimes are guilty of expecting more from our children?**

I recall a situation that occurred when my oldest son was in high school. God used it as a wake-up call, bringing attention not only to my son's sin but also to my own unrealistic expectations.

I discovered he had been out drinking with some friends and went berserk: "What were you thinking? Christians don't behave that way!" I followed with the worst accusation yet, "Who are you? Are you leading some kind of double life?"

At the time, my son was an officer in the Fellowship of Christian Athletes and a leader among his peers in the youth group. The friends with whom he was caught drinking were also leaders in the youth group and a few were even ministry staff kids. In the days that followed the discovery came discussions about the behavior and, of course, consequences for his actions.

"If you have made mistakes, there is always another chance for you. For this thing we call 'failure' is not the falling down, but the staying down."[15]

– Mary Pickford

After the dust had settled a bit, my son and I sat alone at the kitchen table and I asked him, "Why did you do it?"

His simple response? "Mom, I was just curious what it felt like to drink. I know it was wrong, and I wish I had a better answer. But I don't. I was just curious." When he spoke those straightforward words, a lightbulb went off in my head: "Well whadda ya know? My son is a big, stinkin' sinner just like me!"

God used the situation to remind me of a truth I have already mentioned in this study and often teach: "Sin is not a behavior but a condition." Behaviors can be modified, but conditions must be cured. And praise God, we have a cure for the sin condition!

# PERSONAL reflection

Describe a time when you may have set the behavioral expectations bar too high for your children. Why do you think so many parents share this tendency?

It is also possible to set the bar too low. Training our sons in the way they should go requires a tough balance, and it often leaves kids feeling like they don't measure up to their mothers' standards, many of which Mom fails to meet herself. Just like our sons, we moms could use frequent good doses of God's grace and mercy!

GOD'S TAKE on the issue

The Bible offers no shortage of men and women who—like us—struggle in the battle to live by the Spirit rather than by the flesh. I have always taken great comfort in Paul's honesty and transparency over his own struggle with sin.

Read Romans 7:15-23. How well do you relate to verses 17 and 18?
  ● Perfectly   ● Somewhat   ● Not at all
(Note: If you answered "Not at all," we have a big problem!)

BRINGING IT home

Describe a recent situation in which you struggled to do the right thing. Did you "desire to do what is good"?

While we aren't told in the account of David's sin with Bathsheba whether or not he struggled with conviction over his actions, I can't help but think the "desire to do what is good" was tucked away in his heart. He was, after all, ripe for repentance when confronted by Nathan, which indicates a struggle had already taken place within his soul. While it's better never to sin at all, we all do.

Now that we've established that the struggle to live by the Spirit and not by the flesh presents a lifelong battle, I want to talk about a rarely discussed aspect of David's story. It offers wisdom in helping our sons win the battle over temptation and involves a small but critical detail mentioned in the first verse that introduces the account of David's sin.

Read this verse and underline the phrase that follows "Rabbah."
"In the spring when kings march out [to war], David sent Joab
with his officers and all Israel. They destroyed the Ammonites and
besieged Rabbah, but David remained in Jerusalem" (2 Sam. 11:1).

At a time when kings went out to battle, David stayed in Jerusalem. One commentary writer makes the following observation: "[In choosing to remain behind] David omitted God's laws. Had he been now at his post at the head of his forces, he would have been out of the way of this temptation. When we are out of the way of our duty we are in the way of temptation."[16]

Before David committed the sin with Bathsheba, he omitted his personal responsibilities and, more importantly, spiritual disciplines that had once been a part of his daily life. Sins of omission almost always precede sins of commission.

Which spiritual disciplines do people tend to omit?

Prayer	Bible Reading	Fellowship
Worship	Service	Fasting
Obedience to God's Word		

How might failing to spend time with God and neglecting to connect with other believers lead to sin?

WRAPPING IT up

Our sons are more likely to cave to temptations when they are out of the way of their duty. In other words, we need to keep these boys busy doing things that *matter*. Show me a boy who has an absence of spiritual disciplines and too much time on his hands and I assure you sin will soon show up. I'm not suggesting that our sons shouldn't be allowed down time to enjoy certain pre-approved leisure activities, but balance is key. Our sons enjoy great benefits when we provide them with a steady diet of Christian activities that will encourage them to live by the Spirit and not by the flesh.

What do you do to ensure that your son is exposed to a Christian environment and influences?

In what ways do you cultivate spiritual disciplines in your son's life?

Mastery over sin begins with the ability to own sin and respond with a godly sorrow that leads to repentance. I'm so thankful God included the story of David's downfall in His Holy Word. It certainly gives us hope that in spite of slip-ups it is still possible to be men and women after God's own heart. Take a few moments to reflect on the truths God spoke into your heart this week. How might these new insights change the way you parent your son?

CONVERSATION 3

"Not everyone's doing it!" (And other truths about sex you won't hear in the locker room.)

VIDEO GUIDE

Our sons are growing up in a culture that assumes everyone will have sex outside of marriage. It's up to us to make sure they know what God has to say about sex.

Be _____ without robbing your sons of their innocence. For example, "You may be hearing this word at school. We want to talk to make sure you have the information God wants you to have."

In 1 Corinthians 6:13-20, Paul presents the why behind God's command to save sex for marriage.

Verse 18 suggests a solution to escaping the temptation.

The two will become one flesh:
Genesis 2:24; Matthew 19:5; Mark 10:8; Ephesians 5:31

Oxytocin = _____ _____

Sex outside of marriage short-circuits God's design for sex.

CONVERSATION STARTERS with your group:

Describe the plan you have in place to educate your son about God's standards for sex.

Jot down a few possible transition statements to lead into a discussion about sex.

Interested in reviewing this or other 5 Conversations Bible study sessions? You can download all digital sessions by going to www.lifeway.com/women

WEEK 3
Saying No

Plato
~

"Abstinence is the
surety of temperance."[1]

LOCKER-ROOM LIES

let's talk **While researching this book, I stumbled on the following question a young man anonymously submitted to a secular online advice forum geared to teens and young adults: "Should I feel terrible for being a 21-year-old male virgin?"**

He went on to explain, "I really want to have sex with someone I love. I can't seem to get myself to have sex with a drunk girl at a party, [like] everyone else my age … . Both of my girlfriends ended up breaking my heart after a few months, shortly after I told them I was a virgin. It was like they suddenly got uncomfortable and awkward around me …

"I have to lie to all my friends about being a virgin. I feel so pathetic and like a complete loser. Is it normal for me to still be a virgin at 21?"[3]

Sadly, at some level our sons will be exposed to the popular mentality in our culture that male virginity garners suspicion rather than respect. In truth, the young man who submitted the question to the advice forum stands a much better chance of one day enjoying a better sex life than his nonvirgin friends. That is, if he can wait it out.

A study by the National Institute for Healthcare Research found that couples who don't sleep together before marriage and who are faithful during

"When a person has sex, they're not just having it with that partner, they're having it with everybody that partner has had it with for the past 10 years."[2]

- Otis Ray Bowen, MD

marriage are more satisfied with their current sex life (and also with their marriages) compared to those who were involved sexually before marriage.[4] Clear benefits to waiting exist, but you won't hear them touted by the media or discussed in the locker room.

What factors do you think might contribute to the negative mentality regarding male virginity?

CONVERSATION boosters

Using the study findings of the National Institute for Healthcare Research, write a sample dialogue you might have with your son. Debate the popular mind-set that encourages premarital sex and compares it to test-driving a car before you buy.

I wonder how many young men might choose to abstain if they knew their reward would include a higher likelihood of a lasting, monogamous, and sexually satisfying marriage. (What guy doesn't want to have the best sex life possible?) Unless we expose the faulty thinking behind the culture's free-sex message and the fallout that results from believing it, we'll find it impossible to adequately address the issue of sex outside of marriage.

It's not enough to tell our sons to "wait because God says so." It would be nice if it were that easy. The truth, however, is that the message that God created sex for the confines of marriage often gets drowned out by raging hormones, peer pressure, and a nonstop cultural message that "everyone's doing it." And don't forget the delay in the frontal lobe of our boys' brains that limits their ability to link their actions with long-term consequences! No doubt, we face an uphill battle.

My youngest son attended public school and a private Christian school during his high-school years. I asked him about the locker-room mentality regarding the guys committed to waiting. He very matter-of-factly answered, "At both schools, guys brag about having sex; but at (name of his private school), the guys don't really make fun of you if you say you're waiting. They're like, 'yeah, that's cool.'" Naively, I hoped to hear that a good number of the guys were committed to waiting, but such is our world.

The truth is our sons will face the same pressures as other young men and are susceptible to believing the same lies. Unless, that is, we take the time to break down the lies and challenge the mentality that everyone is doing it. A poll reveals that at that time nearly half of high-school students haven't had sex and among those who have, nearly two-thirds regret it and wish they had waited.[5]

Why is it that the students who have sex are considered the norm? Why won't the media give attention to the other half who haven't had sex and even highlight some of the benefits they find in waiting? Ah yes, sex sells, but it's up to parents to sell a different kind of message.

When was the last time you heard the media talk about the approximately 10 million new cases of sexually transmitted diseases (STDs) that occur among young people ages 15-24 in the United States each year?[6] Or that approximately 40 percent of sexually active teen girls are diagnosed with an STD every year?[7] (A statistic that has a direct impact on your son should he decide to have sex.) But STDs aren't the only possible physical consequence of sex outside of marriage.

Six in 10 pregnancies involving teen fathers end in a birth, which is guaranteed to change the entire trajectory of a boy's life. Author Pam Stenzel in her book *Sex Has a Price Tag: Discussions About Sexuality, Spirituality, and Self Respect* reports, "A teen father will end up paying a total of between $50,000 and $250,000 (depending on his income) over the next 18 years" to support a child.[8] Stenzel recounts the following story involving a young man she met while doing a high-school event:

> A few years ago, I spoke at a high school in northern Minnesota. When I was done, a popular senior guy stood up and admitted to his classmates for the first time that he was a dad. The summer before he'd had sex with a girl whose family had been vacationing in the area. They had had sex once. Neither of them thought they'd see the other one again. They had no plans beyond having a good time one night during summer break.
>
> He worked at a Burger King in town. Money was taken out of each paycheck to help support his baby. That will continue at every job he has for the next 18 years.[9]

Stenzel ended by posing this question to the teen guys in the audience: "Guys, what will you say to the girl you want to marry someday if you already have a child? 'By the way, honey, for the next 10 years, a chunk of my take-home pay will be used to provide for my first child, so we're going to have to stick to a tight budget.'" Food for thought and certainly something we need to share with our sons in an effort to help them better understand the long-term physical consequences of sex outside of marriage … even if the sex occurs just one time.

Sadly, our sons will be exposed at some level to the rampant mentality in our culture that male virginity equals a suspicious lack or even personal failure. In a recent survey of 1,200 teen and young adult males (ages 15-22) conducted by *Seventeen* magazine and the National Campaign to Prevent Teen and Unplanned Pregnancy, 78 percent of those surveyed agreed there was "way too much pressure" from society to have sex.[10] Interestingly, the survey also found that guys are not being altogether honest about their sexual experience.

Among the findings:

- 60 percent said they had lied about something related to sex
- 30 percent lied about how far they have gone
- 24 percent lied about their number of sexual partners
- 23 percent claimed not to be a virgin when they were (like the guy I referred to at the beginning of this lesson)[11]

As mothers, we are wise to inform our sons to take the locker-room banter they hear from other guys with a grain of salt. Guys who feel a need to lie in regard to their sexual experience suffer from low self-esteem and are trying desperately to fit in and gain acceptance with the wrong group of guys.

Ironically, many of the guys who mock and tease other guys for being virgins aren't any more sexually experienced than the ones they are teasing! Our sons need to steer clear of guys like this, instead finding a handful of friends who are committed to their values and beliefs.

GOD'S TAKE on the issue

Read Romans 8:5-6. Which two types of people does it describe?

The original Greek word translated with the term "flesh" or with the phrase "sinful nature" is *sarx*; and while the verse is a general reference to those who chase after sinful desires, one of the definitions includes "those who are on the search for persons with whom they can gratify their lust."[12] When it comes to fulfilling their sexual desires, our sons hardly need to go in search of a willing party to gratify their lust. I am not placing blame on aggressive girls but rather making the point that remaining sexually pure will prove a constant battle for our sons.

For this reason, we must approach the topic of sexual purity as a conversation that will be ongoing throughout their growing-up years. Gone are the days of covering the topic with a one-time conversation.

What reward does Romans 8:6 mention for those whose minds are controlled by the Spirit?

What results will the man who lives by the flesh find?

The word *death* is not used in a physical sense, but rather, in a spiritual one. It describes the absence of life and peace.

PERSONAL reflection

Recall a time in your life when sinful actions led to an absence of life and peace.

When talking to our sons about the fallout that can result from premarital sex, we need to make sure they understand one thing. The temporary satisfaction they may achieve in fulfilling the lust of their fleshly nature cannot begin to compare to the satisfaction that comes from experiencing the life and peace that comes from obeying God.

Which of the following might bring a sense of "life and peace"?

____ Not having to worry about STD infection or telling a future partner about having an STD

____ Not having to worry about an unplanned pregnancy

____ Not having to face the possibility of early marriage and/or child support as the result of a pregnancy

____ Knowing that the decision to wait pleases God

____ Knowing that waiting makes a healthy investment in a future marriage

____ Knowing that waiting increases the chance of a more satisfied sex life in marriage

____ Not having to deal with the conviction that comes from sinful choices and the resulting impact on a relationship with God

All of these are benefits to saving sex for marriage. By the time your son reaches the teen years, it's a good idea to address the cultural and locker-room lies to which he will likely be exposed and to present him with the truth: Following God's will for sex and saving it for marriage brings life and peace. And who after careful consideration doesn't want life and peace both now and in the days to come?

Close by praying that your son will recognize the benefits associated with saving sex for marriage. And remember … it's your job to point them out!

SEX IS GOOD ...
VERY, VERY GOOD!

let's talk

When talking with our sons about sex, we need to approach the topic with boldness and confidence rather than skittishness and timidity. We also need to make sure we present it with balance, always remembering that God created sex for His purposes (procreation) and our pleasure (in marriage).

> "How beautiful you are and how pleasing, O love, with your delights!"
>
> - Song of Songs 7:6, NIV

As mothers, we need to be careful not to go overboard in our conversations by always emphasizing the problems associated with sex outside of marriage. In other words, we need to leave our sons with a clear understanding that sex in the right context (marriage) is a good thing and something God wired us to desire and enjoy.

If we fail to acknowledge that sex is, in fact, a gift from God, our sons may be left with the impression that sex is bad, even in marriage.

In the book *Hooked*, authors Joe S. McIlhaney, MD and Freda McKissic Bush, MD note, "Sex can be considered one of the appetites with which we are born."[13] They go on to point out that the word *appetite* can be defined as "any of the instinctive desires necessary to keep up organic life" or "an inherent craving."[14]

A truth to remember is that appetites are *necessary* but values-neutral. They can be used appropriately or they can be misunderstood and misused. For example, without an appetite for food, we wouldn't survive. Food provides energy and fuels our bodies. Yet the misuse of this natural appetite in the forms of overeating or eating too much of the wrong things, for example, can cause problems such as cardiovascular disease, diabetes, and many others. These health problems can dramatically change the entire course of an individual's life.[15]

We need to make sure our sons understand that while their appetite for sex is normal and natural, it is also something that needs to be properly managed in order for them to experience optimum spiritual, emotional, and physical health over the long term.

PERSONAL reflection

Do you recall either of your parents talking to you about sex in your growing-up years?

If your answer is yes, did your parent(s) approach the topic from a balanced point of view, presenting the fallout of premarital sex while emphasizing it as a wonderful gift from God intended for marriage?

If no, what impact (if any) did this have on your view of sex?

How well do you rate yourself on sharing God's plan for sex with your son (assuming he's old enough to hear it)?

I've done a great job. He's got the message.	I've hinted at it a time or two. He'll figure it out.	What? I'm supposed to talk about God and sex in the same conversation?	I can't discuss sex with my son. I get embarrassed reading about it.

I love the simple 1-2-3 approach that sexual abstinence expert Pam Stenzel takes in her book, *Sex Has a Price Tag: Discussions About Sexuality, Spirituality, and Self-Respect*. It offers a great beginning point when your child is ready for the initial conversation and provides a springboard for further talks.

1. **Humans did not create sex, God did.**

2. **Since God created sex, He's the one who understands it the best.**

3. **Since God understands sex better than anyone, a person who wants to have great sex (and why would anyone want to have rotten sex?) needs to know what God says about sex.**[16]

GOD'S TAKE on the issue

So, what does God say about sex?

Read Genesis 1:27-28. What is the purpose of sex in this verse?

Read Proverbs 5:18-19. What purpose do these verses assign sex?

God created sex for procreation (in marriage) and enjoyment (in marriage). The entire book of Song of Songs celebrates the progression of an intimate romance that begins with an initial attraction and is fueled by desire and longing. The romance culminates with a wedding, where the two finally become one.

One commentary states it this way:

> The Song of Songs is a beautiful picture of God's "endorsement" of physical love between husband and wife. Marriage is to be a monogamous, permanent, self-giving unit, in which the spouses are intensely devoted and committed to each other, and take delight in each other. "For this reason a man will leave his father and mother and be united to his wife, and they will become one flesh" (Gen. 2:24). The Song of Songs shows that sex in marriage is not "dirty." The physical attractiveness of a man and woman for each other and the fulfillment of those longings in marriage are natural and honorable.[17]

Our sons need to know that sex is good and that God, the Creator of sex, put some rules in place so that they might experience the best sex life possible. Once your son is clear on the basics regarding the purpose of sex and God's view of it, you now have a foundation to build on in future conversations.

A good rule of thumb to remember when it comes to discussing sex is to keep the conversation simple and keep it going. Take advantage of teachable moments along the way, especially those that send a contradictory message about sex.

CONVERSATION boosters

Describe a recent example from television, movies, or music that exposed you to a message about sex that runs contrary to God's plan and purpose for it.

Imagine that your son was exposed to the same faulty message. What could you say to take advantage of the teachable moment? Write a brief script to use when faced with a similar situation.

I believe that somewhere between the ages of 10 and 12, before they hear otherwise from undependable sources, children should be given a basic definition of sex by their parents. Some moms and dads wait for a signal from the child before they begin the conversations about sex. This is a bit risky since some kids are quieter than others and may shy away from bringing their questions about sex to their parents.

You know best when your son is showing signs of readiness, but I would highly recommend that you begin initiating the conversations about sex before he enters middle school or at the first signs of adolescence, whichever comes first. This is especially true if your son is in a public school or has an older brother or sister and, by default, has been exposed to more mature topics. However, don't let that be your only barometer.

One mom recently shared about her sheltered eight-year-old son (the oldest of three children) who snuck onto the family computer and Googled™ "What is sex?" Her husband discovered the search when checking the computer history, and they were stunned to learn that the word *sex* had somehow made it onto their son's radar. When they asked their son where he first heard of the term, he matter-of-factly told them, "From my friends."

Handling the topic presents a tedious balance because, while we want to protect our sons' innocence for as long as possible, they need to hear accurate information about sex before they are misinformed from outside sources.

Has your son (if he is young) expressed a curiosity about sex or asked any questions indicating it might be time to hold at least a basic birds-and-bees talk? If so, explain.

When I felt it a good time to broach the topic with my sons, I said something like:

Hey buddy, I need to talk to you about something very important. At some point in the next few years, you are going to hear things about sex from maybe your friends or on TV or somewhere else. (This assumes your son has been given a basic definition of the word *sex* by this point. If not, you'll need to add that to your conversation!)

Here's the deal. Some things you will hear aren't true, and I want you to know what God has to say about sex because He's the One who created it. So, make me a promise, please. If you hear something, I want you to come and talk to me or to Dad, OK? Deal?

I followed by asking my son what, if anything, he had heard anything about sex and made sure he knew it was a safe topic to discuss with us. And yes, both of my boys admitted they had already heard something about it from other sources. Thus our conversations began.

We moms must approach the topic of sex with confidence and assurance, so our sons are left with no doubt that it is an amazing gift from God. If we'll only ask, God will give us the wisdom to know when to initiate conversations about sex and the boldness needed to approach the topic with confidence. Our boys need to hear the truth.

SEX ON THE (BOY) BRAIN

let's talk **If your son has hit the first wave of puberty, you've probably experienced the pantry stare-off: You walk into the kitchen and find your boy standing in the entry of the stocked pantry mumbling, "I'm staarrrvving." About the same time his appetite kicks into high gear and your grocery bill goes up, his body begins going through changes at warp speed.**

These changes also leave him "staarrrvving" for sex. I know that's an uncomfortable thought, but we must face the facts if we want to understand the challenge our boys face.

A boy's sudden appetite for sex is fueled by a deluge of testosterone that literally floods his system during puberty. The only other time a boy experiences a testosterone wash of this nature and magnitude happens in utero when the embryo receives a "testosterone bath" during the sixth week of gestation, compliments of the Y chromosome delivered by his father.[19]

In their book *Raising Sons and Loving It!* Gary and Carrie Oliver wrote, "During this testosterone wash the level of testosterone is ten to twenty times stronger in boys than in girls. The ... adolescent boy will have between five to

"Anybody who believes that the way to a man's heart is through his stomach flunked geography."[18]

- Robert Byrne

seven surges of testosterone per day—an increase marked by a tendency to masturbate frequently, be moody and aggressive, want more sleep, lose his temper more often, be negative and critical, act like his head is in the clouds, and have a significantly greater interest in sex."[20]

> How might this information help a mom cope when her little boy morphs into a man-in-the-making?

> If your son has entered the adolescent years, have you witnessed a shift in his behavior? In what ways?

In the book *Making Sense of the Men in Your Life*, author Kevin Leman says, "Men reportedly think about sex an average of thirty-three times per day, or twice an hour. Some people say women think about sex only once a day—when men ask for it."[21] (Sounds about right!) Now, try to imagine how difficult it must be for our sons (and husbands) to be sexually pure when they live in a world all too happy to take advantage of their sexual hunger pangs. Author Rick Johnson adds:

> At the risk of perpetuating a stereotype about men, there's a distinct possibility that if women knew how and what men really think about, they would refuse to be in the same room with them (I use the term men, but it's interchangeable with boys from early adolescence on). They'd think them perverted. Guys think about sex all the time. Men even think about sex in the most inappropriate places, such as in church or at funerals. The slightest and most innocent thing—a

woman's laugh, the curve of a shapely leg, certain shoes, perfume, and thousands of other scents, sights, and sounds—can set men off. During adolescence, when hormones are raging, these stimulations are intensified.[22]

For those of us who are married, it is sobering enough to associate the above information to our husbands, much less our sons. Say it isn't so!

GOD'S TAKE on the issue

Read 1 Thessalonians 4:1-7. Verse 2 explains that the instructions given on how to live were given on the authority of Jesus Christ.

> For what purpose were these instructions given?
> ____ To help us learn how to micromanage our lives
> ____ To turn us into super Christians
> ____ To teach us how to avoid sexual immorality and to live holy lives
> ____ To keep us from ever having any fun

> What instructions are given in verses 3-6?
> ____ Avoid sexual immorality.
> ____ Just do it!
> ____ Learn to control your body.
> ____ Don't give into passionate lust like the heathen.
> ____ Practice makes perfect.
> ____ Do not take advantage of fellow believers.
> ____ Hooking up never hurt anyone. Just make sure you use protection.
> ____ Sex is natural. Just look at the animals—we can't help ourselves.

A sharp contrast exists between the instructions given by God and the messages our sons receive from the culture. A closer look at verses 4-6 as presented in the King James Version provide an interesting insight our boys need to hear: "Every one of you should know how to possess his vessel in sanctification and honour;

Not in the lust of concupiscence, even as the Gentiles which know not God: That no *man* go beyond and defraud his brother in *any* matter: because that the Lord is the avenger of all such, as we also have forewarned you and testified" (emphasis by author).

The word *vessel* in verse 4 refers to a wife. In verse 5 the Greek word for lust is *pathos*, meaning "a feeling which the mind suffers, an affection of the mind, emotion, passion; passionate desire."[23] The word *concupiscence* sheds light on which kind of lust the passage discusses since the Greek meaning of the word is a "desire (specifically) for what is forbidden."[24] But here's where it gets interesting.

Look again at 1 Thessalonians 4:4-6 (KJV), printed for you on pages 87-88. Fill in the blanks to summarize the specific counsel this passage offers men:

Know how to _____ your vessel so that you don't

_____.

To defraud someone means "to gain or take advantage of another, to overreach."[25] When a young man pursues premarital sex or sexual activity, he "defrauds" his partner of what God intended for sex, as well as defrauding his future wife! I would also argue that a young man who engages in sexual activity outside of marriage defrauds himself. In other words, premarital sex is a rip-off for all parties involved.

BRINGING IT home

As mothers we need to take care not to make testosterone a villain and convey to our sons that their appetite for sex is abnormal or unnatural. It is not. However, as the First Thessalonians passage notes, sexual desire comes with great responsibility and must be controlled.

As we discussed yesterday, Song of Songs celebrates sexual longing and desire. It speaks of sex as a by-product of love and more importantly, as something reserved for marriage. However, it gives a caution about love and the sex that accompanies love.

Write Song of Songs 8:4 (NIV). Add "and sons" after the word *daughters.*

I love that God included Song of Songs in the Bible. Had He not done so, many might believe that He created sex solely for the purpose of procreation. God wired our bodies to desire sex, but He intended that we act on that desire only in the marriage relationship.

Sex is a reward of love … love that leads to marriage. Unfortunately, in today's world sex has become independent of love. The world addresses that sex is, in fact, an appetite; but it endorses the mentality that no limits or boundaries exist in satisfying that appetite. Our sons must be taught that sex and marital love go hand in hand.

Recently, my husband walked in the door after work while I was in the kitchen trying to get dinner ready. Our youngest son sat nearby watching TV. Keith always hugs me and gives me a quick kiss when he comes in the door after work. On this particular evening, he came from a business meeting and was dressed in his suit (not an everyday occurrence) and looked exceptionally handsome (Translation: he was smoking hot!).

When he walked over to give me a hug, I said, "Well, hey there, handsome. Whatcha doing later tonight?" To this my son let out a grumble and said something to the effect of "Just kill me now. Get a room, guys."

That wasn't the first time my son (or his older siblings) had been exposed to such remarks. And while they may act embarrassed, we know we have left them with the clear impression that sex within the confines of marriage (as God intended) is a gift.

More importantly, we have connected sex to marital love. Hopefully, we have left them wanting to hold out for the best sex possible. Recreational sex cannot hold a candle to the kind of intimacy God intended for us to enjoy in marriage.

PERSONAL reflection

Imagine your child as a young adult. Suppose someone asks him to describe his parents' view of sex. What might he say based on the attitude you and/or your husband have projected?

If your son had to choose one of the following words to sum up his impression of sex based on your attitude toward his father, would he say sex was a duty or a desire?

If you answered "duty," how might you ensure that your child know sex is a gift from God that is "desired"?

I realize that some women will consider this a painful or complicated topic. If you are married and put sex more in the duty category than the desire category, I highly urge you to take steps to remedy this problem. We need to help our sons see the vital link between sex and marital love in spite of what the world tells them.

A GET-AWAY PLAN

let's talk

Last week we took a close look at how King David's momentary lack of self-control led to a tangled web of sin that led to a lifetime of painful consequences. We discussed how his downfall began with a simple glance from his rooftop on a post-nap walk.

I speculate that David—the man after God's own heart—was familiar with Job's story and his covenant "not to look lustfully at a girl" (Job 31:1, NIV). Further, he knew the high regard God places on marriage. But while David surely had an escape plan for dealing with temptation, he chose not to use it.

Our sons need more than a pep talk on self-control if we want them to fight the temptation to have sex: They need an escape plan. While we cannot make them use such a plan, we can educate them on the need to have one and pray they will put it into practice when temptation strikes. Notice I said "when" temptation strikes. Whether sexual temptation comes is not a matter of if, but when; therefore, we are wise to help our sons prepare for it in advance.

Of course, this assumes that they want an escape plan and are committed to sexual purity. If your son has conformed to

> "In reading the lives of great men, I found that the first victory they won was over themselves ... self-discipline with all of them came first."[26]
>
> - Harry S. Truman

the ways of the world and you suspect he is already sexually active or resistant to the idea of abstaining from sex, you need to start at square one and cover the material presented over the past few days. He won't likely see the merit in having an escape plan until he is aware of culture's lies and becomes convinced of the benefits of waiting.

PERSONAL reflection

Describe a tempting situation you managed to escape.

Recall a time when you succumbed to some type of temptation.
Can you recall any warning signs that preceded your fall?

- Yes
- No
- Ugh, I'm starting to squirm here.

How might your response to the tempting situation have been different had you developed an escape plan ahead of time and heeded the warning signs on the front end?

We all sometimes stumble for lack of a plan. Does this make it easier to extend grace to your son when he slips?

- Yes
- No
- OK, you got me. I need to do a better job of extending grace.

According to the study *Forbidden Fruit: Sex and Religion in the Lives of American Teenagers* by professor of sociology Mark Regnerus, "Evangelical teens don't accept themselves as people who will have sex until they've already had it."[27] Regnerus continues, "For evangelicals, sex is a 'symbolic boundary' marking a good Christian from a bad one, but in reality, the kids are always 'sneaking across enemy lines.' "[28] Certainly this is a humbling thought for well-meaning Christian parents, many of whom unfortunately can relate to sneaking across enemy lines in their own teen years.

And therein lies the problem. If our children don't expect to have sex, they aren't prepared to address the temptation to have sex. And if we don't expect them to have sex, we won't prepare them to resist the temptation. But the truth is, a good number of church kids are having sex.

Half of all mothers of sexually active teenagers mistakenly believe that their children are still virgins, according to a team of researchers at the University of Minnesota Adolescent Health Center.[29] For most Christian parents, the extent of the "sex talk" boils down to "God says you should wait until marriage to have sex." Period. End of sentence and discussion. No escape plan offered … just a one-time very brief talk.

GOD'S TAKE on the issue

First Corinthians 6:18 encourages believers to flee from sexual immorality. "Every sin a person can commit is outside the body … but the person who is sexually immoral sins against his own body." The Greek word for flee is *pheugo*, meaning "to run away."[30] While it's unlikely that our sons will physically run away from sexual temptation, we need to help them think through reasonable ways to remove themselves from tempting situations.

What reason does the passage give for fleeing sexual immorality?

The Message presents 1 Corinthians 6:18 this way: "There is a sense in which sexual sins are different from all others. In sexual sin we violate the sacredness of our own bodies, these bodies that were made for God-given and God-modeled love, for 'becoming one' with another."

God promises our sons two things regarding temptation.
According to 1 Corinthians 10:13, what are they?

God will not allow our sons to experience a temptation that cannot be mastered. In fact, those who end up mastered by a sin either failed to (1) have an escape plan or (2) implement a previously established escape plan. In Conversation 2, I mentioned the delayed growth in the frontal lobe of the boy brain, which can make it difficult for our sons to connect consequences with actions.

When it comes to sexual temptation, our sons must learn the basics of self-control before their hormone surge kicks into high gear and the word *flee* fails to get on their radar screen. This is why it is so important to teach principles of self-control at a young age. Impulsive toddlers grow into impulsive teenagers, who frequently grow up to be impulsive adults.

We need to teach our sons that the most effective way to flee temptation is to steer clear of tempting situations in the first place. (Recall the STP model of Stop, Think, and Pray in the Conversation 2 DVD session.) The second line of defense? To recognize and heed the warning signs. When those two steps fail, boys need a back-up (or escape) plan.

Let's say, for example, that your 17-year-old son is in a dating relationship. His girlfriend sends him a text asking him to come over and study. She follows this text with, "My parents will be gone for the next few hours. :)" Obviously, it's much easier for your son to flee at this point (by exercising self-control and choosing not to place himself in a tempting situation) than to head to his girlfriend's house and attempt to exercise self-control in the middle of a make-out session.

And should a similar temptation come with no warning, our sons need to think through what they might say in order to escape it before such a need arises.

BRINGING IT home

Write your ideas for such an escape plan and pray that your boy will be receptive to God's command to flee when he faces temptation.

YOU'RE #1!

let's talk **Study after study confirms a direct link between engaged, caring parents and children making wise choices. Don't ever doubt the power you have to influence your son when it comes to sexual purity.**

One study indicated that teenagers in grades 8-11 who perceive that their mother disapproves of their engaging in sexual intercourse are more likely than their peers to delay sexual activity.[32]

In addition, The National Campaign to Prevent Teen Pregnancy conducted a survey that questioned 1,000 young people ages 12 to 19 and 1,008 adults age 20 and older and found that 45 percent of teens said their parents most influence their decisions about sex compared to 31 percent who indicated their friends are most influential.[33]

Another study found that teenagers who "feel highly connected to their parents and report that their parents are warm, caring and supportive—are far more likely to delay sexual activity than their peers."[34]

"Nothing makes it easier to resist temptation than a proper bringing-up, a sound set of values—and witnesses."[31]

- Franklin P. Jones

Additional research found that close relationships with mothers seemed to discourage youngsters from sexual activity.[35]

Sarah Brown, director of the National Campaign to Prevent Teen Pregnancy, notes that talk alone is insufficient. What matters most, especially among younger teenagers, is a relationship in which parents keep close tabs on them, knowing who their friends are and what they do together.[36]

GOD'S TAKE on the issue

Ephesians 5:1-17 provides an excellent blueprint for addressing the culture's lies.

Summarize the following verses into a five-step action plan:

1. 5:1

2. 5:3

3. 5:6-8

4. 5:11

5. 5:15-17

What sort of parental boundaries might you need to establish to help your sons live out verses 3, 4, 6, and 7?

Remember, your voice will be the loudest voice your son hears—even if it appears he's not listening. One survey found that 88 percent of teens said it would be easier to postpone sexual activity and avoid teen pregnancy if they were able to have more open, honest conversations about the topic of sex with their parents. That's certainly good news for those of us who are willing to speak up. Sadly, the same study found that only 32 percent of parents surveyed believe they are most influential in their teens' decisions about sex.[37] We must help our sons make the vital connection of why God wants them to save sex for marriage. As we help them build a proper foundation based upon the truth set forth in His Word, we equip them to defend against the culture's lies.

I realize some of the statistics presented this week may leave you with a heavy heart. As mothers who desperately want what's best for their sons—in this situation, saving sex for marriage—second best just doesn't seem good enough. But while I pray my sons will experience God's best when it comes to His plan and design for sex, ultimately, the decision to wait is theirs—not mine. Our sons possess free will, and many will learn some truths the hard way. That doesn't mean that they are beyond God's reach or, for that matter, His grace. No guarantees or foolproof formulas exist when it comes to raising sons who pursue sexual purity, even for those of us writing the parenting books.

And while it is reasonable to have high expectations for our sons, we need to be careful that we don't send a message to our boys that anything less than perfection (in this case, saving all sexual activity for marriage) is unredeemable. I'm not suggesting we present the topic of sex from the perspective that they are most likely going to give into the temptation. As with most anything, balance proves key.

Read each passage and write its prescription (Rx) for avoiding sexual temptation. I've done the first one for you.

Psalm 119:9
Rx: Stay focused on God's Word.

Psalm 119:59
Rx:

Proverbs 14:15
Rx:

2 Timothy 2:22
Rx:

BRINGING IT home

I can honestly say I have fulfilled my assigned role in consistently talking to my sons about the fallout associated with premarital sex as well as the benefits of saving sex for marriage. I've taken advantage of teachable moments when we sit at home, walk along the road, lie down, and get up (see Deut. 6:7). Should my sons decide to forego God's best for sex in spite of my teaching and instruction, I will rest in knowing I did the best job I could and will continue to pray that their hearts would be sensitive and ripe to God's teaching.

I recently told my youngest son, "It's your sex life, son, and ultimately, you have to come to the conclusion that saving sex for marriage is in your personal best interest and promises the healthiest sex life possible—emotionally, physically, and spiritually. Bottom line, you have to care more about your sex life and the pursuit of godly purity than I do."

Can you imagine having a similar conversation with your son when
he hits the teen years?

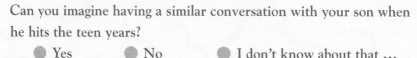 Yes   ● No   ● I don't know about that …

If you didn't answer yes, explain.

We need to raise boys who are in the habit of daily laying their hearts bare before God. They may experience slip-ups along the way, but it is their response to those slip-ups that matters most to God. When we help our sons cultivate the habit of guarding and protecting their hearts, we address sexual purity at the root.

Should our sons be among the rare few who can lay claim to being a virgin on their wedding day, it will not be the direct result of any trendy formula or parenting strategy we employed. It will happen by God's grace alone. Fortunately, that same grace is also available to those who slip up along the way. I am living proof that God's grace covers a multitude of sins and has the power to make all things new.

Close by praying that your son will choose sexual purity and that God will give you the strength and boldness to break down the culture's lies and replace them with God's amazing truth.

CONVERSATION 4

"Boyhood is only for a season. P.S. It's time to grow up!"

_____ ____ _____ syndrome:
"Boomerang kids" or "Peter Pans who shave"

Corporations and marketers are being encouraged to
consider the often-overlooked 25-to-34-year age group
as part of the _____ _____.

What's a mother to do?
We must have a _____ _____ ____ _____ in which
we're purposeful about moving our sons from one stage to the next.

Pre launch: ages 2-12   Introduce them to skills of _____
_____, money management, goal setting

Test launch: ages 13-18   More independence, _____
_____they have been taught, assuming ownership

Final launch: ages 19-22   Increasingly _____,
entering workplace or college or military

1 Corinthians 13:11
Manhood is a state in which childishness should have
become _____.

CONVERSATION STARTERS with your group:

What steps are you currently taking to launch your son into adulthood?

WEEK 4

Launching Manhood

F. Scott
Fitzgerald
~

"[Growing up] is a terribly hard thing
to do. It is much easier to skip it and
go from one childhood to another."[1]

BOYHOOD: ONLY FOR A SEASON

let's talk **Over the years I've encouraged my daughter to hold out for what I call "a top-shelf kinda guy." During her college years she expressed disillusionment over the shortage of godly, mature college men and claimed that very few seemed headed in a provider, protector, and spiritual leader ("top-shelf kinda guy") direction.**

"Unless we rely on God's power within us, we will yield to the pressures around us."

- Unknown

She confirmed what many studies already report: Boys do have a hard time growing up. Oh sure, the words *mature* and *college guys* aren't typically used together in the same sentence; but by late college, most girls hope to see among their male peers at least a glimmer of the desire to mature.

As graduation nears, many young men seem more content with building their fantasy football teams than building careers and families. And mind you, these are the church guys I'm talking about!

As the mother of two sons, I hope my boys are the kind of young men mothers dream about their daughters marrying—the kind of young men who know how to man up. There are some good guys out there, but very few prove great and godly.

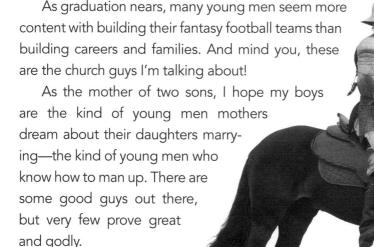

This begs the question: How can we raise "top-shelf kinda guys," those who resist the culture's pressure to conform to their surroundings and seek to live instead by God's standards? Today we'll focus on four young men in the Bible who stood out among their peers and earned the "top-shelf kinda guy" label.

Read Daniel 1:1-7. Why do you think the boys' names were changed?

The finest and most intelligent young men of Hebrew nobility were taken as slaves. Stripped of names meant to honor God, the young men were given new titles meant to honor Babylon's gods as they began preparations to serve the pagan king. The name change and training were geared toward wiping home out of their minds. A steady diet of Babylonian language, culture, and delicacies could have driven all thoughts of Israel's God out of their hearts.

Interestingly, The King James Version uses the word *children* instead of *youth* when describing the young Israelite men. At first glance, getting out from under Mom and Dad's watchful eye and living with your best buds might sound like a perk to the average teenage boy. However, it's safe to say Babylon provided a stark contrast to the upbringing of most of the Israelite young men. This new setting had to leave them somewhat rattled. Exposure to an environment with an opposing value system can lead to a culture shift and uncertainty.

In what situations might your son experience this type of shift?

I remember when my oldest son received his roommate assignment in the summer before his freshman year in college. Excitedly, he looked up the name of his roommate on Facebook® while I sat beside him. Imagine our shock when we discovered his roommate was not a fellow freshman but a returning junior with a vast collection of party pictures. I was having a hard enough time sending my son to a college more than 800 miles from home, but seeing a photo of his future roommate puking into a dorm toilet about did me in. I couldn't dial the student housing number fast enough! (Helicopter mom? Guilty as charged, but no regrets!) Even though I was able to correct the roommate situation, I remember how helpless I felt at the thought of what might lie ahead.

> If your son has ever been exposed to a Babylon-like environment, describe it. What, if any, impact did it have on him?

Read Daniel 1:8-16.

In this passage the young prophet and his three friends took a moral stand that reflected an important difference in their lives. One Bible commentary notes:

> Without doubt this royal food had been sacrificed and offered to pagan gods before it was offered to the king. To partake of such food would be contrary to Exodus 34:15, where the Jews were forbidden to eat flesh sacrificed to pagan gods. Similar problems would arise in drinking the wine. To abstain from the Old Testament prohibition against "strong drink" (e.g., Prov. 20:1, KJV; Isa 5:11, 'drinks'), Jews customarily diluted wine with water. Some added 3 parts of water to wine, others 6 parts, and some as much as 10 parts of water to 1 part of wine. The Babylonians did not dilute their wine. So both the food and the drink would have defiled these Jewish young men. Daniel knew the requirements of the Law governing what he should and should not eat and drink.[2]

> How do you think Daniel knew the requirements of the Law?

How might knowing what is expected of them before they leave our care help our sons to navigate life on their own?

Daniel and his three friends had been uprooted from their homeland, family, and all that was familiar. Yet they remained steadfast in their faith.

What did the other Israelite boys do in regard to the proposed menu?

___ Graciously declined and asked for Daniel's Daily Special of water and veggies

___ Asked if they could run home for a quick home-cooked meal

___ Pigged out! We're talking gourmet food and undiluted wine here!

No doubt most young men raised in church would opt for the king's food if they found themselves facing a similar challenge. Would your son be among them? Or would your son cling fast to his faith?

BRINGING IT home

What can you do to more proactively equip your son for the Babylon-like environments he is sure to encounter? Check all that apply.

- Get him to church every time the doors open.
- Lock him in his room.
- Encourage and model daily Bible study.
- Pray with him regularly.
- Openly encourage him to obey God's ways despite the world's opinions.
- Freak out whenever he does something wrong.
- Insist that every T-shirt he wears has a Christian theme.
- Vocally praise his positive choices, and draw attention to what he does right.

In Daniel 1:19 the king assessed the four young men who chose honoring God over their stomachs: "No one was found equal to [them]. So they began to serve in the king's court. In every matter of wisdom and understanding that the king consulted them about, he found them 10 times better than all the diviner-priests and mediums in his entire kingdom" (Dan. 1:19-20). Sticking to what they learned in the early years helped them survive and excel when confronted with the unfamiliar.

Over the following years these young men held fast to their faith while their peers conformed to their surroundings. For Daniel and his friends, the choice came with blessing, but refusing the king's food was only a warm-up for the challenges that were ahead.

The ongoing pressure to conform is similar to the challenge our sons face today. But just as Daniel and his friends found approval and later advancement from standing against the tide, our boys too can benefit from the determination not to become like their environment.

Meg Meeker, author of *Boys Should Be Boys*, says:

> The biggest mistake we make with adolescent boys is forgetting that they all need help moving *out* of adolescence. Millions of boys grow older, but few become men. No boy really wants to stay in the banal world of perpetual adolescence, but he needs someone to lead him out. His deepest longings pressure him toward manhood, and he needs to respond. He wants to respond but he simply doesn't know how. So help him. Be there to challenge him. Make him a little uncomfortable by stretching his intellect and demanding maturity.[3]

This begs the question: What constitutes an official "adult"? While financial independence (no supplemental income/housing from parents) is an obvious determinant, the pursuit of marriage and parenthood were once viewed as benchmarks. My husband and I worked hard to help our sons move out of adolescence, preparing them to be providers, protectors, and spiritual leaders. Much of what we will discuss during this week is related to the launch plan we used with our sons.

It's our responsibility as parents to make sure our boys are grounded in the right value system before they find themselves facing a culture shift. "Top-shelf kinda guys" are made, not born. Pray that your son will stand firm in his faith and uphold the values you've taught him rather than conform to the world's attitudes.

MONEY MATTERS

let's talk **When my oldest son went to college, my husband presented him with a contract. (He's an attorney, so contracts are part of his love language!) My husband and I hold to the philosophy that college serves as the final phase in the launch to adulthood. This runs in stark contrast to the popular mind-set that college serves as the season to sow one's wild oats (and essentially, conform to the culture).**

"If a man is lazy, the rafters sag; if his hands are idle, the house leaks."

- Ecclesiastes 10:18, NIV

We believe college is a privilege and not a right; therefore, we expect a return on our financial investment. After tallying up the approximate dollar amount our son's four-year education would cost, we sat him down for a meeting.

We explained that there were plenty of other ways we could put our money to good use. In other words, we weren't paying (insert dollar amount) to see him show up in pictures on Facebook playing beer pong at frat parties. We reasoned that should that be his desire, he could go to the local community college, find an apartment, and get a job to pay for it.

In addition to expressing certain academic, moral, and spiritual expectations (find a local church to attend weekly), we also required him to work in the summer months to earn money for his yearly recreational expenses. Also, he had to manage

his income and expenses; if he ran out of money before the end of the month, he was out of luck.

That said, my son grew well acquainted with Ramen noodles! We also made it clear that we would only underwrite four years of college, which served as a motivating factor for him to graduate on time. As it was, he graduated in 4½ years; as per the contract agreement, he was required to take out a personal loan to finance his final semester.

While such a contract may seem rather harsh, it worked well for our son, and we have since used the same tactic with his younger two siblings. We didn't expect perfection so we extended some grace along the way; but overall, we couldn't be more proud of the results and of our son! Ironically, he graduated while I was in the process of writing this week's material. He has a job lined up and is engaged to be married: a successful launch into adulthood.

In the book *Boys Adrift,* author Leonard Sax shares a letter he got from a single woman who addresses the growing problem of the "failure to launch" syndrome so common among young men today:

> Dear Dr. Sax,
>
> As a 29-year-old woman, I'm smack in the middle of the "failure to launch" generation. … I went to my 10-year high school reunion last year. All of the girls I went to school with have moved out, gone to college, [and] gotten real jobs. Almost all the boys live at home, have menial jobs, and don't know what they want out of life. … The girls have discipline. The boys have PlayStations®.[4]

 **PERSONAL** reflection

How would you feel if by his 10-year high-school reunion your son matched the profile of the type of man (boy) described by the woman mentioned above?

GOD'S TAKE on the issue

Read 2 Thessalonians 3:6-12. What warning does verse 6 give?

Rate the importance we should place on instilling in our sons a strong work ethic.

We should make it a high priority.	We should suggest they consider it.	We should let them figure it out on thier own.

What reason did Paul give for the hard work they performed (v. 8)?

_____ They were vying for the "apostle of the week" title, which included preferred parking for the winner's camel and a framed certificate to hang on the wall.

_____ They didn't want to be a burden by depending on others to meet their needs.

_____ They wanted to earn enough overtime pay to afford a new gaming console releasing the following week.

The Message words verse 8 this way: "We didn't sit around on our hands expecting others to take care of us. In fact, we worked our fingers to the bone, up half the night moonlighting so you wouldn't be burdened with taking care of us." I love that word picture of someone "sitting around on their hands" while others scurry around taking care of their needs.

Explain how we see a similar picture among young men today.

Write the simple rule or command given in 2 Thessalonians 3:10.

One Bible commentary had this to say about verse 10: "There is here a reference to the sentence pronounced on man in Paradise in consequence of disobedience: 'In the sweat of thy face shalt thou eat bread' (Gen. 3:19). Labor, indeed, may in one point of view be considered as part of the curse, but it is also a blessing adapted to man's fallen nature. Labor is the law of God; idleness is the parent of many crimes and is productive of misery."[5]

Explain how labor can be a blessing.

In what ways can idleness parent crimes and produce misery?

For at least 50 years, the statistical pattern has increased of more women than men attending college (58 women for every 42 men), with "male students … significantly less likely to earn high honors or to graduate."[6] While motivation and other factors related to work and future success do differ, we can make some assumptions. "Because we still see some of these successful young men around us, it's easy to miss the reality that more young men than ever are falling by the wayside."[7]

Deep within the soul of every man, I believe, is a desire to work for a living, independent of the help of others. I believe this same desire is felt even among the men whose wives out-earn them. Men are wired by God to provide for their families. When they fall short of that, they feel less like the men God intended.

Read 1 Timothy 5:8.

How does God view this type of young man?

Let me clarify: not every young man is cut out for college. A *Time* magazine article addressing the problem of delayed adulthood among men reported a surge in apprenticeship programs that give high-school graduates a cheaper and more practical alternative to college.[8] Our culture tends to assume that every youth is entitled to a college education, and many parents have adopted that attitude. The truth is that some youth are better suited for vocational jobs or the military.

I have several friends who discovered that college was not a good match for their sons when their boys landed back on their doorsteps within the first year. One friend's son has since joined the military, and another friend's son is attending community college and working part-time. Not every young man takes the same path to adulthood. The point, however, is that every young man should do what he can to earn his way.

Allowing our sons to live indefinitely off our support does them no favors, and it certainly won't help their future wives. As we close today, ponder some ways you can encourage a strong work ethic in your son's life.

THE BEAUTY OF MARRIAGE

let's talk *Time* magazine recently ran an article titled "Who Needs Marriage? A Changing Institution." The piece cites daunting new statistics from a study conducted by the Pew Research Center, which discovered a shift in attitudes surrounding marriage.

For example, in 1960 approximately 70 percent of American adults were married; now that number is down to about half. Eight times as many children are born out of wedlock today as then. In the 1960s, two-thirds of 20-somethings were married; in 2008 only 26 percent were.[10]

The Pew study, in association with *Time* magazine, conducted a nationwide poll and found that 4 in 10 of those surveyed say marriage is becoming obsolete. The poll also found that a whopping 44 percent of Americans under 30 believe marriage is heading for extinction.

"What we found," the researchers reported, "is that marriage, whatever its social, spiritual or symbolic appeal, is in purely practical terms just not as necessary as it used to be."[11]

"There is no more lovely, friendly, and charming relationship, communion, or company than a good marriage."[9]

- Martin Luther

The institution of marriage is in great need of a positive PR campaign. Many young people are beginning to buy the lie that marriage is a curse, not a blessing.

In an article discussing the shifting attitudes toward marriage, theologian and author R. Albert Mohler, Jr. offered this reminder: "Christians see marriage, first of all, as an institution made good and holy by the Creator. Its value, for us, is not established by sociology but by Scripture. We also understand that God gave us marriage for our good, for our protection, for our sanctification, and for human flourishing. In other words, the Bible compels us to see marriage as essential to human happiness, health, and infinitely more."[12]

GOD'S TAKE on the issue

Reflect on Dr. Mohler's statement that "the value of marriage is not established by sociology but by Scripture." How do you think God feels about marriage? (Bonus points if you can provide a Bible verse!)

Read Genesis 2:18-24. In spite of being placed right smack in the center of a paradise on earth, Adam was missing something: a female helpmate.

How might Genesis 2:18 refute the common message peddled to our youth to look out for number one, putting one's self above all else?

In spite of the negative attitudes that surround marriage, most teens still say they expect to marry (77 percent of boys; 84.5 percent of girls); further, the majority lists "having a good marriage and family life" as "extremely important."[13] Unfortunately, our young people will hear little about the benefits of marriage.

When was the last time you heard the media address the overwhelming and consistent findings by such reputable sources as the *Journal of Marriage and Family* and *The American Journal of Sociology* that married persons, both men and women, are on average considerably better off than all categories of unmarried persons (never married, divorced, separated, and widowed) in terms of such aspects as happiness, satisfaction, physical health, longevity, and several other aspects of emotional health?[14]

Given that God created marriage, should it really come as a surprise that marriage is, in fact, good for us? Happy marriages require commitment and hard work, but the payoff is worth it.

In Genesis God built this case for marriage: It is not good for man to be alone. Then, throughout Scripture, He reveals an even higher purpose for marriage other than a cure for man's loneliness and a means to populate the earth. God intended marriage to paint a beautiful picture of the covenant He made with His people.

Read 2 Corinthians 11:2 and list the marriage-related words you see.

God uses the marriage union to draw a parallel to the covenant relationship He has with His people as well as the relationship Christ has with the church. How important, then, is marriage to God?

- It's a pretty big deal.
- He can take it or leave it.
- It won't matter if it's extinct in 10 years.

Mothers, it's up to us to extol the benefits of marriage as a God-ordained union that can bring much happiness to us and honor to Him. The National Marriage Project states that the burden of changing attitudes about marriage rests with parents. "Contrary to the popular notion that the media is chiefly responsible for young people's attitudes about mating and marriage, available evidence strongly suggests that young people get many of their ideas and models of marriage from parents and the parental generation."[15] That's the good news.

The bad news is that the same study also found that "many parents have had almost nothing good to say about marriage and often say nothing at all," claiming the negativism and/or silence could be due to "the parental generation's own marital problems and failures."[16] Many in the study grew up with unhappily married or divorced parents. These young people have no baseline for determining what a healthy marriage looks like. Some described a good marriage as "the opposite of my parents'." Ouch. Moreover, a number of participants in the study said they received "no advice" or "mainly negative advice" about marriage from their "parents and relatives."[17] That last statement should cause a collective shudder.

BRINGING IT home

> What steps might you take to offset negative attitudes about marriage perpetuated by the culture so that your son might develop a better impression of marriage as defined by God?

No doubt, many reading this have experienced hurt and pain in marriage. For the sake of our sons, however, we must put aside any negatives we may have personally experienced in marriage and focus on God's purpose for it. In the book *Boys Should Be Boys*, physician Meg Meeker notes:

> The most important decision a man makes in his life (aside from ultimate questions about God) isn't choosing his college, his career, or what city he's going to live in. It's choosing his mate. If a man's marriage is good, life is good. He can lose his job, a child, a home, but if he has a solid relationship with a spouse, he draws strength from it to endure the hardships. If, on the other hand, the relationship is tumultuous and painful, life feels bad. His job leaves him feeling less satisfied, his interests in hobbies wane, and he is more likely to give up hope in all other areas of his life. One of the greatest gifts we can give our boys is preparation for marriage.[18]

Close by praying for a new and improved campaign for marriage. Ask God to reveal to you the influence you have in developing or changing your son's attitudes about marriage.

MARRIAGE-BUSTERS

let's talk **Recently I spoke with a Christian mother who has two children in college. During the course of the conversation, she mentioned that she hopes her son "will not do something stupid like get married right out of college."**

I asked her why she felt marriage would be a stupid move and she replied, "You're only single once" and expressed hope that her son "will wait until his late 20s or early 30s and enjoy his single years while he still can."

Can't marriage be an enjoyable experience too, I wondered. And what about saving sex for marriage? Did she really expect her son to wait that long? I'm certainly not suggesting that every young man is ready for marriage upon graduating college; but as believers, we need to examine the double standard we place on our sons by embracing the culture's trend of delayed marriage while at the same time expecting them to remain pure.

Given that most boys begin to have sexual urges in the late adolescent or early teen years and the average age of marriage for men is now 27 or 28,[20] is it really reasonable to expect Christian young men to successfully fight off their sexual urges for a decade and a half? (If you said yes, you might want to go

> "Don't marry the person you think you can live with; marry only the individual you think you can't live without."[19]
>
> ~James C. Dobson

back and review the information we discussed in Session 3 about the male appetite for sex.) Of course, it's possible to remain pure until your late 20s or older, but is it likely?

William Doherty, Director of the Marriage and Family Therapy Program at the University of Minnesota and a professor of Family Social Science, agrees we send a contradictory message to our children when we preach abstinence while also agreeing with societal pressures to delay marriage. "From a traditional moral and religious standpoint, if you want to discourage premarital sex, you really need to be encouraging earlier marriage," he advises.[21] As a disclaimer, he is not endorsing teenage marriages, noting they are risky. He points out that "when you get into your twenties, those teen risks go away."[22]

In a thought-provoking essay addressing the problem of stunted maturity among men, author Frederica Mathewes-Green states, "God designed our bodies to desire to mate much earlier, and through most of history cultures have accommodated that desire by enabling people to wed by their late teens or early twenties. People would postpone marriage until their late twenties only in cases of economic disaster or famine—times when people had to save up in order to marry."[23] While there are valid reasons to marry later, we may want to reexamine the benefits of marrying in the early twenties. I find it ironic that many young people delay marriage in an attempt to reduce the chance of divorce; yet in reality, it actually increases their chances of experiencing a failed marriage. Mathewes-Green notes: "Fifty years ago, when the average bride was twenty, the divorce rate was half what it is now, because the culture encouraged and sustained marriage."[24]

GOD'S TAKE on the issue

Read the following verses. What common theme or buzz words do they share?

Proverbs 13:6   Proverbs 14:8   Proverbs 15:21

Consider the feasibility of our sons postponing marriage and sexual temptation until 30 or so. Circle whether you think it reasonable or folly in God's eyes.

Not surprisingly, a report entitled "The State of Our Unions" by the National Marriage Project found that "a prolonged period of single life may habituate men to the single life. ... They have become accustomed to their own space and routines. They enjoy the freedom of not having to be responsible to anyone else." In addition, the report found that "men see marriage as a final step in prolonged process of growing up."[25] William Doherty, of Minnesota's of the Marriage and Family Therapy Program, cites a cultural shift as the cause for this new attitude of delayed marriage: "We've become more individualistic, living for our own pleasure—not for duty and responsibility. People have this feeling that they owe themselves a decade to have fun before settling down."[26]

> Given the finding discussed yesterday—that married people are
> typically happier than unmarried people—what hazards might those
> who delay marriage find?

While many Christian parents fail to talk with their adolescent and teenage children about the importance of saving sex for marriage, even more fail to warn against cohabitation. Sadly, for many parents, the topic doesn't even make the radar until after their children leave home and they find themselves faced with the reality of the situation—as in the case of minister's wife I know whose virginity-pledging daughter (now in grad school) recently dropped the bomb that she is moving in with her boyfriend because "times have changed" and "everyone does that now." We must devote ourselves to discussing the impact of cohabitation with our children before they leave the nest.

Read Hebrews 13:4.

At first glance this verse appears to address the specific sin of adultery, but it actually speaks of honoring marriage and keeping the marriage bed pure. When our sons save sex for marriage, they are honoring their future marriages. While most of our culture would agree that adultery is wrong, many find nothing wrong with living together outside of marriage. God sees no distinction between the two. In fact, The Message paraphrases Hebrews 13:4 this way: "Honor marriage, and guard the sacredness of sexual intimacy between wife and husband. God draws a firm line against casual and illicit sex."

The King James Version is more blunt: "Marriage is honourable in all, and the bed undefiled: but whoremongers and adulterers God will judge." Yikes, the Bible certainly doesn't sugarcoat the problem! Clearly, God does not take the sin of cohabitation lightly, nor should we. Reminding our sons of this fact is the first step to breaking down the culture's lies regarding cohabitation.

What was once considered immoral and unacceptable has now shifted into somewhat of an expectation, especially among men. The study by the National Marriage Project found that most participants view cohabitation in a favorable light, and almost all the men agreed with the view that a man should not marry a woman until he has lived with her first.[27] Nearly 70 percent of those who get married lived together first.[28]

What's the reasoning behind the decision to shack up? Included are the three most common cited by unmarried singles: (1) They hope to find out more about the habits, character, and fidelity of a partner. (2) They want to test compatibility, possibly for future marriage. (3) They want to live together as a way of avoiding the risks of divorce or being "trapped in an unhappy marriage."[29]

Take the cohabitation quiz to test your knowledge.
Circle (T) for True or (F) for False.

T F Cohabitation increases the risk that the relationship will break up before marriage.[30]

T F Studies find that those who live together before marriage have less satisfying marriages.[31]

T F Those who live together before marriage have higher separation and divorce rates.[32]

T F Those who go on to marry their cohabitation partner or someone else are more likely to have extramarital affairs.[33]

T F Married people have both more and better sex than do their unmarried counterparts.[34]

You made a perfect score if you answered each statement "True." The verdict is in: Living together before marriage can impact the health and welfare of our sons' future marriages.

CONVERSATION boosters

Given the facts presented in the quiz, how might you refute the culture's attitude regarding cohabitation in the following situations?

1. You walk through the living room and discover your teenage son watching a popular sitcom. The lead couple is living together outside of marriage (certainly not an uncommon theme in TV land!).

Your response:

2. A relative plans to stay overnight at your home during the holidays and is bringing his girlfriend along. They live together and assume it will be OK to share a room while staying with you.

Your response:

3. Your son graduates from college and gets engaged to his long-time girlfriend. The economy is tough. Rather than pay two leases for a short six-month period before the wedding, they announce that

they are planning to move in together. They both were raised in the church, but claim it's "just not that big of a deal."

Your response:

The best time to educate your son regarding the sin of cohabitation is before he's capable of cohabitating. Never assume your son will not be among those who fall prey. My friend was shattered when her daughter and her fiancé subscribed to the line of faulty thinking in scenario 3. Though her daughter was active in the church and a leader in Fellowship of Christian Athletes and took great pride in saving herself for marriage, she conformed to more popular opinions regarding sex and marriage after only a few short years at a liberal university.

Given the high percentage of couples who live together before marriage, it's clear she is not alone; a large number of proclaiming believers have conformed to the ways of the world. Over lunch one day, my friend expressed regret over failing to discuss cohabitation and having had only a handful of conversations related to premarital sex and marriage: "I just assumed she was on board because she had signed a virginity pledge and knew it was wrong."

Take a lesson from my friend's experience. Arm your son with the truth related to God's plan and design for marriage. Not everyone will go on to marry, but most will. Therefore, it is irresponsible not to address the topic of marriage with our sons and make sure they are clear on matters related to God's view of marriage. Honoring the marriage bed begins now.

End today by praying that God will equip you with everything you need to teach your son to honor marriage and to protect his future marriage by making wise and God-pleasing choices.

GROWING UP IN THE FAITH

let's talk **I can still remember the freedom that came when each of my children moved from the bottle and strained baby foods to a cup and solids. We could take them to restaurants without having to pack up the diaper bag with baby food. Chances were good that we could find something on the menu to cut up and put in front of them so they could feed themselves.**

I remember when my youngest son had his first taste of peanut butter. It was love at first bite. One of my favorite home movie clips features him as a toddler when he managed to somehow convince his older sister to fetch a jar of peanut butter that was out of reach in the pantry while I was upstairs taking a shower. The mess I came upon when I entered the kitchen was indescribable.

I'm not sure if any of the peanut butter made it into his mouth, but it was in plenty of other places! It covered his face, hair, clothes, and unfortunately, everything he touched during my brief absence. Because he was the third child, my first instinct was to get out the camcorder and film the damage rather than have a minor melt-down, which would have been my response had our firstborn pulled the same stunt.

"Oh, to have a church built up with the deep godliness of people who know the Lord in their very hearts, and will seek to follow the Lamb wherever he goes!"[35]

- Charles Spurgeon

The command in Proverbs 22:6 to "teach a youth about the way he should go …" denotes a process that occurs over years. Just as our kids need us to wean them off milk and toward solid food, so too are they dependent on us to initially spoon-feed them in matters of faith.

The goal is to raise our children to be grounded in God's truths so they'll eventually seek Him on their own in all matters of life. We often forget, however, that our children don't go from being spoon-fed to neatly feeding themselves without getting a little messy.

Just as was the case with my son's first attempts to feed himself a handful of peanut butter, spiritual progress doesn't always look tidy and neat. But messy or not, progress is still being made.

Write 1 Peter 2:2-3 here, describing how one matures spiritually.

These verses remind us that spiritual maturity is a process that occurs over time. Just as we are to prepare and train our sons in skills to help them become financially independent, so are we also called to disciple and train our sons to become spiritually independent.

Verse 3 suggests the foundation for spiritual growth: "tasting" or rather learning for one's self that "the Lord is good." My son loved peanut butter because he had tasted it and determined it to be good stuff. Therefore, he desired another taste. And another. Where did he get his first taste? From the very grown-ups who cared for him!

How can you help your son "taste" that the Lord is good?
Circle all that apply.
 a. Share with him stories of how God has helped you.
 b. Explain how God listens when we pray.
 c. Insist that you are right in every situation and never say, "I'm sorry."

    d. Bring up biblical examples that apply to situations he faces,
       encouraging him that God cares and understands his struggles.

    e. Point out his every bad behavior, contrasting it with the righ-
       teousness we should strive to reach.

    f. Expose him to other Christians whose lives reflect God's love
       and biblical values.

Choices *a*, *b*, *d*, and *f* are great examples of how we can help our sons taste that the Lord is good. The Greek word for good is *chrestos*. It means better, easy, gracious, and kind. Unfortunately, many children grow up in homes where they get a minimal or light taste of the Lord, but not enough positive exposure to Him to leave them craving more. Sadly, this can inhibit spiritual growth.

PERSONAL reflection

Describe a situation in which someone you know grew up in a Christian home and later turned his or her back on the faith due to experiences that left a bad taste.

How might the situation have turned out differently if the individual had been better acquainted with the Lord's kindness and goodness?

It's interesting that "easy" is one of the words supporting the Greek word for "good."

Read aloud 1 Peter 2:2-3, substituting the word "easy" for "good."

Those of us who sampled the world's delicacies and can testify to the bitter taste they leave, might have an easier time understanding how the Lord's ways are "easy," comparatively speaking. Among a mother's deepest desires is the hope that her children will not repeat some of her own mistakes—the same mistakes, mind you, that helped lead her to her own conclusion that the Lord is, in fact, good and that His ways are, in fact, easy.

Often, we expect our church kids to know better and to make a perfectly seamless transition in the journey along the road to spiritual maturity. As I reflect back on all three of my children's spiritual journeys, they each experienced times where they wandered for a time from God's path. They were still going to church and doing church things, yet they were somewhat stagnant in their faith. It's a scary process for a parent to watch and one that will most certainly build your faith (and extend your prayer time!).

GOD'S TAKE on the issue

Read Hebrews 5:11-14.

The writer of the Book of Hebrews aired his frustration with the Hebrew people's inability to understand the deeper truths he presented. In verse 11 he suggested that at the root of the problem lay the fact that they no longer tried to understand, while some translations such as the NIV use the term "slow to learn" or "dull of hearing" to describe their problem. No doubt that description accurately describes many of our sons, especially when they are playing video games and we remind them to take out the trash!

The apostle's frustration stemmed from the fact that those he was addressing had already learned the basics and should be teaching others. In a nutshell, he told them to "grow up" in their faith.

In Hebrew 5:13-14 the apostle made a clear distinction between infants and those who are mature. What is it?

One Bible commentary notes:

It is unsatisfactory to remain a baby in spiritual matters. This is true because a spiritual infant, living on milk ... is not acquainted with the teaching about righteousness. The words "not acquainted" (*apeiros*) might be better rendered "inexperienced." It is not so much that a spiritual "infant" lacks information—though at first he obviously does—but rather that he has not yet learned to put "the teaching about righteousness" to effective use. He lacks the skill which goes with maturity and which results in the ability to make appropriate moral choices. Such ability is exactly what is possessed by those who … have trained themselves to distinguish good from evil. That kind of person can handle solid food.[36]

Our sons can't achieve spiritual maturity and the blessings that come with it until they learn to train themselves to distinguish good from evil. As mothers, we are called to act as trainers in our sons' lives, helping them learn discernment and encouraging them to put it into practice. In Week 2 we focused on teaching our sons principles of self-control and the importance of living a Spirit-filled life. We must remain vigilant in the task to move our sons beyond milk and onto solid food.

BRINGING IT home

Read 1 Corinthians 3:1-3.

In verse 2 Paul offered great wisdom regarding the way he presented spiritual truths to the people of Corinth that can help us in the way we approach the spiritual training of our sons. Simply put, he spoke to them at a level they could understand.

In verse 3, what did Paul mention as the cause of their spiritual immaturity?

In Week 2, we discussed mastery over sin and the discipline of self-control. Spiritual maturity is not possible unless or until our sons recognize the power of sin in their lives and thus, their need of a Savior.

Matthew Henry's Commentary states it this way:

> It is the duty of a faithful minister of Christ to consult the capacities of his hearers and teach them as they can bear. And yet it is natural for babes to grow up to men; and babes in Christ should endeavor to grow in Stature, and become men in Christ. It is expected that their advances in knowledge should be in proportion to their means and opportunities, and their time of professing religion, that they may be able to bear discourses on the mysteries of our religion, and not always rest in plain things.[37]

As the commentary notes, we are wise to adjust our teaching to our sons' level of understanding and to teach as they can bear. We can't expect our boys to respond to life's challenges at the same spiritual level of maturity we currently possess. If we set the bar too high and offer little room for error, we set our sons up for failure and frustration.

Rather than seeing that God is good, they might get the impression that God's a hard taskmaster who doesn't understand that life is difficult. At some point, however, it may be necessary to lovingly confront them if "their advances in knowledge" are not "in proportion to their means and opportunities" (much like the apostle's tough-love conversation in Hebrews 5:11-14).

If your son has been on milk for a while, the most loving thing you can do is to challenge him to move on to solid food. I doubt many of us would allow our sons to head off to grade school with a Ziploc™ bag of Cheerios™ and a baby bottle packed in their lunch bag. Why then would we allow our boys, who have grown up in the faith on a steady diet of solid food, to remain spiritual infants? If we want to successfully launch our sons into the world to become the godly men God created them to be, we must do our part to help guide them toward maturity.

Ask God to help you honestly assess your son's spiritual maturity (if he is old enough to understand the concept of sin and God's forgiveness). Should he be showing more evidence, given the "diet" you have provided him? If so, it may be time to lovingly confront him. The truth is we cannot make our children "grow up" spiritually, but we can make it clear that it was never God's intent (or ours) for them to remain infants in the faith.

CONVERSATION 5

"Godly men are in short supply— dare to become one!"

Times haven't changed much. We still want to raise good boys.

Luke 15:11-32

Goodness doesn't always translate to _____.
We want to raise sons who pursue godliness over goodness.
If we focus on behavior modification rather than heart inhabitation
or examination, we run the risk of raising a Pharisee.

We need to pay attention to the _____ _____ _____ _____
and not just to the outside. Out of the heart are the issues of life.

We need to teach our sons that _____ _____ _____ _____
heart, first and foremost.

Hebrew word for examine is *shaphat* (shaw-fat´), which means to
"judge," as in to pass sentence for or against. The idea of inviting God
to put our hearts on trial can be unsettling.

Remember the father, with both the prodigal son and the elder son,
and his _____, _____ _____. He
was after their hearts.

CONVERSATION STARTERS with your group:

Do you find yourself tending to parent your son's behavior
or your son's heart? How can you tell?

Interested in reviewing this or other 5 Conversations Bible study sessions?
You can download all digital sessions by going to www.lifeway.com/women

WEEK 5

Pleasing God

2 Peter 1:3

~

"His divine power has given us everything required for life and godliness… ."

GOD-PLEASERS

let's talk I recently received an e-mail from Lindsay, a single mom who expressed apprehension in regard to raising a son:

"My marriage was destroyed by infidelity. My concern in raising a son by myself is modeling for him how to be a godly, respectful, and honorable young man. The mom can't model how to be a good man. It's not what is modeled to him by our culture nor unfortunately by his own father.

"I know that God is big enough to overcome that, but raising him to be a man in this culture seems like a daunting task."

We all share Lindsay's desire to raise godly sons, and I greatly admire moms who lack a godly male role model in the home to help bear the task. But Lindsay mentioned an important point in saying that God is big enough to make up for loss, so hang in there if you face a similar challenge. He will help you!

This week we'll address key attributes that will aid us in raising our sons into godly men. One of the greatest challenges they will face in the journey to manhood comes from the world's pull to conform to their surroundings.

"It's never right to do wrong; it's always right to do right. Just because everyone else is doing it, doesn't mean you should."[1]

Michael Catt,
Courageous Living

The apostle Paul addressed a similar concern with the Galatians, offering a warning that we need today.

> Read Galatians 1:1-9 and summarize Paul's concern for the churches of Galatia. Look at verse 6. At what was the apostle Paul "amazed" (HCSB) or "astonished" (NIV)?

Various translations use verbs such as "deserting" and "turning" to explain what so amazed the apostle. The original Greek word Paul used is *metatithaymee*, which means to "transfer, exchange, change sides, or to figuratively pervert."[2] In short, the people were turning their attention away from Christ's teachings in order to go right back to living the world's ways.

I love the image of changing sides. While Paul was specifically addressing the naivety of the Galatians to embrace a perverted form of the gospel, the problem of "deserting" and "turning" surfaces among all believers. The Message paraphrase says it this way: "I can't believe your fickleness—how easily you have turned traitor to him who called you by the grace of Christ by embracing a variant message!"

> Describe a situation in which a believer was fickle and subsequently "changed sides." What were the consequences?

In Galatians 1:10 Paul pointed out that he was not trying to please men but God. Our sons will have a tendency to want to "win the favor of men" (NIV) in an attempt to fit in and conform to the culture that surrounds them. They face a constant pull to live as people-pleasers rather than God-pleasers.

Last week on Day 1 we discussed the bold decision of Daniel, Shadrach, Meshach, and Abednego to forego the food and drink from the king's table. Today I want to look at the fruit that followed their decision to be God-pleasers rather than people-pleasers. In the years after this stand for God, all four men faced life-or-death situations that would again test their faith.

Let's start with Daniel. If your son was raised in church, chances are he knows the story of Daniel in the lion's den. It has been played out on preschool flannel boards, featured in a Veggie Tales™ movie, and taught in Vacation Bible Schools.

In Daniel 6 the Babylonian king decreed that any man who prayed to any god over a 30-day period would be thrown to the lions.

Read Daniel 6:10 and describe Daniel's courageous act.

According to the verse, Daniel knew of the law, yet he prayed anyway. All he had to do was go 30 days without his daily discipline of prayer. Or draw the curtains and pray in secret. Let me ask you a painful question: How many mothers, in a similar situation, would encourage their sons to take the safe, people-pleasing route? How would you respond?

Read Daniel 6:16. What did the king say to Daniel at the time Daniel was being thrown to the lions?

Our goal as mothers is to raise sons who develop the habit to "serve God continually." They just might find that sticking to their faith not only brings unexpected blessing—as proved the case when God sealed the lions' mouths shut—but also heart changes in those persons who observe their lives.

Read Daniel 6:26-28. What new decree did the king issue at Daniel's release?

Shadrach, Meshach, and Abednego also underwent a testing of their faith when King Nebuchadnezzar erected a 90-foot golden statue and commanded all the people to bow down and worship it.

Read Daniel 3:6-15. What sentence could be expected by those who refused to obey this command?

What did Shadrach, Meshach, and Abednego do when they heard the chorus of instruments?

____ Ignored the edict

____ Gave a half-bow in the statue's general direction

____ Prayed to God while falling prostrate before the statue

Contrast their actions with those of everyone else—including the other young Israelite men taken into captivity.

I love Shadrach, Meshach, and Abednego's answer to the king's "last chance" offer in verses 16-18: "Nebuchadnezzar … If the God we serve exists, then He can rescue us from the furnace of blazing fire, and He can rescue us from the power of you, the king. But even if He does not rescue us, we want you as king to know that we will not serve your gods or worship the gold statue you set up." All the three Hebrew men had to do to resume their normal lives was bow to the statue. All they had to do was conform like most everyone else had. Instead, they took an incredible stand for their faith.

How did the king take the news? (See vv. 19-23.)

____ He was not a happy camper.

____ He ordered the furnace turned up seven times hotter than normal.

____ He had his soldiers bind the three young men and toss them in the furnace.

____ All of the above.

Consider the God-pleasing decision these young men made. How might their mutual friendship have played a role in their actions?

Shadrach, Meshach, and Abednego had each other to help build a sense of accountability for their decisions and to encourage one another to stay strong. Our sons likewise need friends who will stand firm in their faith rather than bow down to temptations.

Read Daniel 3:25-30. Describe the outcome of the courageous stand taken by these three men.

CONVERSATION boosters

While it's not likely our sons will face the threat of a fiery furnace or a den of hungry lions, they will face plenty of stand-at-the-crossroads moments where they will have to make the decision: Should I follow God or the crowd?

Consider the following scenarios representing common stand-at-the-crossroads moments that boys face. How could you encourage God-pleasing behavior in each circumstance?

1. Your teenage son landed a great summer job at a movie theater. Unfortunately, it will require him to work most Sundays. When he mentioned to the manager that he attends church regularly, she responded, "Sorry, Bud. Weekends are required. If I make an exception for you, I'll have to make an exception for everyone."

Your response:

2. Your middle-school-age son has a couple of friends from school over, and they are playing a parent-approved video game on the computer in the next room. You overhear one of your son's friends say, "This game is lame. Let me show you a game my older brother plays with his friends."

Your son stammers, "Uh … I don't know. My parents are really picky about the sites I go to and the video games I play." His friend replies, "C'mon. What are you—10 years old?" and begins to laugh.

Your response:

3. Your son, a serious baseball player, tries out for and makes a select team. When the coach announces the schedule, you realize that half of the games are out of town, requiring you and your son to miss church.

Your response:

Each scenario requires parents to react. As moms, we lead by example and can hardly expect our sons to be God-pleasers if our actions don't line up. As we close today, ask God to give your son a desire to please Him. While you're at it, ask God to continually give you the same longing.

A GOOD AND GODLY REPUTATION

let's talk **I once heard a speaker say, "You are who you've been becoming." In Week 2 we discussed a few famous downfalls, noting that they began with a decision to live for the flesh rather than by the Spirit. Tiger Woods, Mel Gibson, and Ted Haggard, among others, have earned reputations based on their downfalls, reputations that will prove extremely difficult to shed.**

"It takes many good deeds to build a good reputation, and only one bad one to lose it."[3]

- Benjamin Franklin

Similarly, our children and teens have a cognitive disconnect when it comes to making choices. They find it difficult to mentally walk a decision down its logical path and weigh all possible consequences. As we teach our sons the biblical principle of self-control, we must also help them understand that their actions determine their character and that their character, in turn, will determine their reputation.

Socrates, 4th-century B.C. philosopher, once said, "Regard your good name as the richest jewel that can possibly be possessed. The way to gain a good reputation is to endeavor to be what you desire to appear."[4] For our sons, "endeavoring to be what they desire to appear" can be a full-time job—especially when added to the challenge of growing up is an Internet that records everything … and forgets nothing.

🌿 PERSONAL reflection

Consider your youth. Had you enjoyed access to the same technology your son has today, how might it have affected your reputation?

Today's technology combined with boys' delayed frontal-lobe development makes me wonder how it's possible for any young man to have a good reputation! The familiar admonition, "Your sins will find you out" has never been more true as around-the-clock, instant access to technology sits at our sons' fingertips.

Case in point: A couple of months ago, someone posted something inappropriate on my youngest son's Facebook wall. When I saw it, I brought it up to my son's attention and reminded him that if I could see it, other "friends"—including his youth minister, third-grade teacher, and his Memaw—could see it too! He dismissed the incident as no big deal saying, "Yeah, but that's not really one of my friends. My real friends don't talk that way, and they know I don't talk that way."

I replied that few reading the comment know that the young man is not one of his good friends and that no one really knows that my son doesn't talk that way. I then explained the principle of guilt by association and told him that he must vigilantly protect his reputation from misunderstandings that can occur based on false assumptions. Unfortunately, such is the world our sons live in today.

CONVERSATION boosters

Read Ephesians 5:1-17, which offers a wealth of wisdom we can use to teach our sons how to guard and protect their reputations. With this passage in mind, create a biblical solution to the following.

1. You decide to spot-check your son's text messages and find an inappropriate message from his friend that includes a derogatory reference about a girl in their grade.

Your response (see v. 4):

2. Your son and a church friend are listening to music on the
   computer in the next room. You overhear his friend telling him
   how to download music for free. When your son asks if it's legal,
   his friend responds, "No. But pretty much everyone does it. It's
   not that big of a deal."

   Your response (see vv. 6-7):

3. You get a call from the father of a young man who attends your
   son's school. He informs you that his son had a party the night
   before (with his approval), but it came to his attention that his son
   and a few other students drank alcohol there. He mentions that
   your boy left the party early and didn't appear to have been drinking, but he felt responsible for calling the parents of the students in
   attendance to inform them of the presence of alcohol.

   You confront your son, and he admits to knowing alcohol was available. He claims he left for that reason. However, he is frustrated
   that his classmate's father felt it necessary to call all the parents.

Your response (see vv. 11-13):

All of these reflect real-life situations that occurred while I parented my own two sons through the teen years! And believe it or not, each scenario involved church kids. We can't assume that every person who attends church has a relationship with Christ, but Ephesians 5:8 offers insight regarding those who claim to be believers.

Summarize that verse here.

Believers are different because we belong to Him, Ephesians 5:8 reminds us. To explain the manner in which Christians should live so that they are easily identified as Christ followers, some translations use the phrase "walk as children of light." The Greek word for walk is *peripateo*. It means to "walk as proof of ability, to deport oneself, to follow."[5] The Contemporary English Version expresses it this way: "You used to be like people living in the dark, but now you are people of the light because you belong to the Lord. So act like people of the light."

In summary, our sons who claim to be believers should act and behave in such a way that they are set apart from nonbelievers. Lives that show little to no fruit among those who claim to be "children of light" should be a great cause of concern. Sure, all believers have times when they stray from God's path and conform to the patterns of the world (Rom. 12:2), but those instances should resemble temporary detours, not a way of life.

If you feel a strong concern for your son's spiritual state, pray. Consider having a blunt conversation about the truths contained in Ephesians 5:1-17.

BRINGING IT home

A good reputation is grounded in a pursuit of godliness. However, a big difference exists between a "good reputation" and a "godly reputation." The key to obtaining both is found in Proverbs 3:1-4:

> "My son, don't forget my teaching, but let your heart keep my commands; for they will bring you many days, a full life, and well-being. Never let loyalty and faithfulness leave you. Tie them around your neck; write them on the tablet of your heart. Then you will find favor and high regard in the sight of God and man."

In order to remember God's teaching, our sons must first know God's teaching. As they grow in the knowledge of it, they must write God's ways and laws on the tablets of their hearts. Then they will be able to pull from those reserves as the need arises. We can do our part to provide them with adequate teaching over the years, but we cannot make them tuck the teaching away in their hearts.

Furthermore, we cannot make them draw on those truths and apply them to their daily lives. We can, however, step up our prayers and ask God to give our sons a love for His commands.

End today by turning Proverbs 3:1-4 into a personal prayer for your son.

RECLAIMING CHIVALRY

let's talk

While most people are familiar with the sinking of the _Titanic_ and the chivalry displayed by many of the men on board, few are aware of the sinking of the _Lusitania_ three years later and more notably, the lack of chivalry displayed during its demise. The _Titanic_ carried 2,207 passengers and crew when it hit an iceberg and sank. The _Lusitania_ carried 1,949 people when it was struck by a German torpedo.

"Some say that the age of chivalry is past, that the spirit of romance is dead. The age of chivalry is never past, so long as there is a wrong left [uncorrected] on earth."[6]

- Charles Kingsley

Strangely, both ships lost about the same number of people: The _Titanic_ had a death rate of 68.7 percent and the _Lusitania_ had a death rate of 67.3.[7]

Attempting to examine how social norms hold up in a time of crisis, a team of behavioral economists decided to take a deeper look into the profile of those who survived on each ship. Their findings

were recently published, and the authors documented several interesting conclusions about human behavior.

Aboard the *Titanic*, children under 16 were nearly 31% likelier than the reference group to have survived, but those on the *Lusitania* were 0.7% less likely. Males ages 16 to 35 on the *Titanic* had a 6.5% poorer survival rate than the reference group but did 7.9% better on the *Lusitania*. For females in the 16-to-35 group, the gap was more dramatic: those on the *Titanic* enjoyed a whopping 48.3% edge; on the *Lusitania* it was a smaller but still significant 10.4%.[8]

Clearly the final scenes onboard the *Lusitania* resembled more of a survival-of-the-fittest scenario. Why then did the younger and fitter males not display the same measure of chivalry as the male passengers on the *Titanic*? The most significant factor was determined to be the time it took each ship to sink. The *Lusitania* sank in a mere 18 minutes; the *Titanic* took 2 hours and 40 minutes. One of the theories presented by the authors conducting the study was that those onboard the *Lusitania* experienced "the short-run flight impulse dominated behavior. On the slowly sinking *Titanic*, there was time for socially determined behavioral patterns to reemerge."[9]

A related article points out that the "theory fits perfectly with the survival data, as all of the*Lusitania's* passengers were more likely to engage in what's known as selfish rationality—a behavior that's every bit as me-centered as it sounds and that provides an edge to strong, younger males in particular. On the *Titanic*, the rules concerning gender, class and the gentle treatment of children—in other words, good manners—had a chance to assert themselves."[10]

Author and theologian Albert Mohler notes that "Aboard the *Lusitania*, young males acted out of a selfish survival instinct, and women and children were cast aside, left to the waves. Aboard the *Titanic*, there was time for men to consider what was at stake and to call themselves to a higher morality. There was time for conscience to raise its voice and authority, and for men, young and old, to know and to do their duty."[11]

Their "duty." I wonder how many sons from Bible-believing homes would understand that it was their "moral duty" as prescribed by God to put the

needs of others, especially those who are weaker, above their own needs …
even if it meant losing their lives in the process.

PERSONAL reflection

Do you desire to raise your son to be the kind of young man who
would surrender his seat without hesitation?

● Yes   ● No   ● I'm not sure

Behind the idea of extending help to the weak is the concept of chivalry.

Circle those words you equate with the term *chivalry.*

Courage	Justice	Piety
Courtesy	Honor	Good manners
Desire to help	Generosity	Defender

If you circled each option, you have a good understanding of what chivalry's all
about. In medieval times, knights lived by the code of chivalry. In the Victorian
era chivalry thrived. Even in our grandparents' generation, men routinely tipped
their hats to ladies and opened doors for women and small children.

How have attitudes about chivalry changed over the past 50 years?
Share an example.

Few would argue that chivalry is on the verge of extinction. In fact, I shudder to think how the *Titanic* scenario would play out in today's society.

Yet, courtesy is a learned skill. When our sons are young, we train them how to get along with others. As they get older, we need to train them to emulate our examples of kind behavior and encourage them to put chivalry into practice in their own lives.

How might you help your son put chivalry into practice now?

CONVERSATION boosters

We cannot expect the culture to train our boys in chivalry. They'll learn largely by watching our interactions. Consider how you would expect your (grown) son to behave in the following situations. Explain what you would do to help him understand what to do in a similar instance.

1. You walk into the grocery store with your son to pick up a few things and see a woman struggling to separate two shopping carts that are stuck together.

   You ...

2. As you leave the store with your son, an elderly woman heads toward the entrance.

You ...

3. You are traveling with your son and board the airport tram to switch terminals. You find a seat, but at the next stop, a woman with two young children steps on and all the seats are occupied.

You ...

What chivalrous acts would you hope to see your son display when dating?

Look over your list and note any items you have not yet addressed with your son—assuming he's old enough to learn. Know that he needs to hear your voice regarding how to best interact with others. Without our direction, it's unlikely our sons will naturally gravitate toward behaving in a chivalrous manner. (P.S.: You may want to discuss unacceptable and rude behaviors that are forbidden in mixed company! His future wife will thank you someday!)

GOD'S TAKE on the issue

Write Philippians 2:3-4 here.

The Message says it this way: "Don't push your way to the front; don't sweet-talk your way to the top. Put yourself aside, and help others get ahead. Don't be obsessed with getting your own advantage. Forget yourselves long enough to lend a helping hand." In a culture where looking out for Number 1 is modeled as the goal, our sons need more examples of people who are willing to "forget themselves long enough to lend a helping hand."

A lack of chivalry is rooted in selfishness while chivalry requires selflessness. Our sinful nature leans toward the former. Only with Christ's help can we even begin to train ourselves to be selfless.

One of the greatest examples of Christlike selflessness and humility is the Reverend John Harper, a 39-year-old widowed preacher who traveled aboard *Titanic* on its fateful voyage. Reverend Harper was en route to preach in Chicago and traveled with his six-year-old daughter and her aunt.

As soon as Harper realized the ship would inevitably sink, he handed his child to her aunt who was already in a lifeboat. He certainly could have pleaded for a spot on the boat and likely earned one, given his little girl had already lost her mother and would be orphaned without him; instead, he trusted the results to God's divine sovereignty and remained behind to help others.

Harper spent the next minutes walking the deck yelling, "Women, children, and the unsaved into the lifeboats!" before plunging into the icy waters when the ship split in two. According to survivors, he swam from survivor to survivor proclaiming, "Believe on the name of the Lord Jesus and you will be saved!" before succumbing to his own death.

Four years later, at a survivor's meeting in Canada, a man recounted through tears that John Harper led him to Christ in the dark Atlantic—just moments before Harper succumbed to hyperthermia and slipped beneath the surface.[12]

Upon hearing this inspiring account of a true gentlemen who modeled a Christlike character rarely seen in today's world, I have to wonder: *Would I be willing to give up my seat on a lifeboat for another woman, child, or for that matter, for someone who doesn't know Christ? Would my sons be willing to do so? Would yours?*

As we close today, pray that God would help us not only raise but also require our sons to be chivalrous toward others. Chivalry may be rare, but it's not yet extinct. It's up to us to keep the tradition alive.

A HUMBLE OFFERING

let's talk **If you have ever spent a few minutes on a social networking site, you've likely witnessed an occasional cocky status update in the newsfeed.**

I recently received a friend request from someone I had not seen in a while, so I clicked over to his profile to get a quick update on his life.

What greeted me was a bio the length of *War and Peace*, one that mentioned just about every achievement in his lifetime. I half expected to see "4th grade Spelling Bee champ" on his never-ending list of accomplishments!

Seriously, the entire thing left me feeling a bit uneasy—and not the least bit surprised that he is still single! Poor guy. Someone forgot to tell him that a little humility goes a long way.

Humility is a vital ingredient when it comes to developing a character of godliness. The Bible has a lot to say about this character trait.

"Humility is to make a right estimate of one's self."[13]

- Charles H. Spurgeon

147

GOD'S TAKE on the issue

Match each reference with the message it shares.

1. Psalm 18:27
2. Psalm 25:9
3. Proverbs 27:2
4. Ephesians 4:1-3
5. James 4:6
6. James 4:10

a. To walk worthy of God's calling on our lives, we should demonstrate humility.

b. God exalts those who humble themselves before Him.

c. God humbles the haughty.

d. God leads the humble and teaches them His ways.

e. Praise over accomplishments should come from others, not our own mouths.

f. God resists the proud but gives grace to the humble.

Which verse most speaks to your heart? Why?

PERSONAL reflection

In your opinion, is it possible to be both self-confident and humble? If yes, how?

In our attempts to raise sons who are self-confident, we must make certain that their confidence is based not on what they've done but on who they are in Christ.

Read Philippians 2:5-8. Whom should we emulate as the ultimate model for humility?

Describe Christ's attitude toward the task He received.

Write verse 8 to summarize Christ's assigned task.

The New Living Translation presents the passage like this: "You must have the same attitude that Christ Jesus had. Though he was God, he did not think of equality with God as something to cling to. Instead, he gave up his divine privileges; he took the humble position of a slave and was born as a human being. When he appeared in human form, he humbled himself in obedience to God and died a criminal's death on a cross."

Wow, if that doesn't take your breath away, I don't know what will. If ever a man had cause to boast and think highly of Himself, it was Christ, the perfect, sinless Son of God. Yet Jesus modeled the ultimate example of humility when He took on the punishment for our sins and agreed to die so that all who believe in Him wouldn't have to face eternal separation from God.

Who, then, are we to boast of anything? Humility is the opposite of pride. It is a constant reminder that we are nothing apart from Christ.

Our sons need to know that the qualities that define a godly man come from hearts humble and submissive to God's leading. Only by His power are we able to quench our selfish tendencies and see others as more important than ourselves. This, of course, is easier said than done.

Read Luke 14:8-11.

I love how The Message paraphrases verse 11 of this passage: "What I'm saying is, If you walk around with your nose in the air, you're going to end up flat on your face. But if you're content to be simply yourself, you will become more than yourself." In other words, if we don't learn humility on our own, we shouldn't be surprised when God takes us down a notch to teach us!

This passage reminds me of a story I heard about a church that formed a committee to find the most humble person in the congregation. Many names were submitted and numerous candidates evaluated. Finally, the committee came to a unanimous decision. They selected a quiet man who always lived in the background and had never taken credit for anything he had done. They awarded him the "Most Humble" button for his faithful service. But when he pinned it on the next day, they had to take it away.[14] While this is not a true story, it illustrates the difficulty of balancing confidence alongside humility.

In Isaiah 66:2 God states that He made all things. Without His creative power, then, nothing—and no one—would exist.

Read Isaiah 66:2. On what three human qualities does God look favorably?

1.

2.

3.

The first quality God mentions in this verse is humility, an attitude that is translated "poor" in some versions. Given the first statement God makes in this passage, humility means to recognize our rightful place. We are here by God's sovereign hand. He created us; therefore, we answer to Him. With humility comes the ability to honestly evaluate oneself through God's lens.

As believers, we should see ourselves as sinners saved by grace. He rescued us from the penalty of sin; as a result, our lives should display humble gratitude. If we do not possess humility, we will lack responsiveness to God's Word.

The second quality God prefers is a contrite or submissive spirit. The Hebrew word for contrite is *nâkeh*, which means "smitten, maimed, dejected."[15] Modern dictionaries explain the concept as "feeling or expressing remorse." Due to our sinful state humans are, in fact, "maimed in spirit." Only God can fix that problem, bridging the gap between sinful humanity and His own holiness.

Third, God looks favorably on those who tremble at His Word. God is looking for those who will approach Him with awe and reverence. He knows that those who are more likely to exalt themselves will be less likely to exalt Him.

Awe of and reverence for God are sadly lacking in our culture.
List examples of how this is the case.

While we can't make our sons express a sincere reverence for God, we can (and should) require them to respect Him while they live under our roofs. You have every right to ban TV shows and movies that blaspheme God or to forbid your children and their guests to use the Lord's name in vain. Teach this principle in a loving manner, patiently explaining the biblical command to "fear the Lord." A healthy respect for God can only help our sons in the quest to grow into wise, productive young men.

Even though true humility stems from the heart, we should not let our sons off the hook just because they don't feel like practicing humility. As with the other qualities we have discussed, we teach our boys spiritual disciplines at an early age and reinforce them over the years in the hopes that these disciplines will become second nature.

Boys taught the spiritual discipline of humility are better equipped to say no to sex outside of marriage, to practice integrity in school and in the workplace, to feed the hungry and clothe the poor, to work through marital difficulties, and to become faithful and productive followers of Christ. Perhaps the best example we can leave our sons to encourage them to behave as the gentlemen God created them to be appears in John 3:30 when John the Baptist—a man whose own name drew crowds—says of Christ, "He must become greater; I must become less" (NIV).

John knew that his mission on earth was not to grow in popularity or to seek increasing fame. He knew that as God's people, we are servants and nothing more. Everything we have—possessions, talents, health—comes from God's hand and belongs to God. This reality includes the wonderful blessing of our sons. They are simply on loan to us for a season.

Close today by writing a prayer. Ask God to help you in the pursuit of modeling and teaching humility to your son. Incorporate the phrase, "More of You, Lord ... and less of me."

WORKS IN PROGRESS

let's talk **I recently ran into an old friend I hadn't seen for some time. She has a son about the same age as my oldest son so I asked how he was doing.**

I could tell by her expression that her words would be seasoned with disappointment: "He's not exactly where we hoped he'd be by now. He dropped out of college and has had a hard time keeping a job. Worst of all, he seems to have turned his back on his faith.

"I keep asking myself, *Where did I go wrong?*" With a shake of her head, her eyes filled with tears before continuing, "I guess the jury's still out. Pray for him."

Where did I go wrong? How many mothers have asked themselves that question as their children disappoint them or stray from the faith? I know I have. I think it's normal to want a sure-fire formula when it comes to this parenting gig we've been given. Deep down, don't we all wish for some sort of guarantee that if we'll just employ a certain set of parenting principles, our children will "turn out"?

And what exactly does it mean to "turn out," anyway? Some parents would define it as "to grow up, get a job, pay your taxes, and stay out of jail." But I imagine most of us have higher

"I don't believe there are devils enough in hell to pull a boy out of the arms of a godly mother."[16]

- Billy Sunday

153

hopes for our sons. We're not in the mom business just to raise sons who simply "turn out" by the world's standards.

We want more. We want our sons to live for Christ and to follow Him for the remainder of their days.

Unfortunately, parenting comes with no guarantees. Sure, we can do things to increase the likelihood that our sons will choose God's path; but in the end, the choice is theirs. The problem is that many of us allow the outcome of our children's lives to tangle with our sense of identity—as in the case of the mother who expressed disappointment over her son's detour from God's path and somehow imagined it was her fault.

How, then, can we explain how another young man with no spiritual influence whatsoever in his home grows into one of the godliest men alive? For all we know, my friend's prodigal son could one day share his own amazing testimony. Our boys are works in progress, and we cannot hold ourselves singly responsible for their outcome.

GOD'S TAKE on the issue

Read 1 Corinthians 3:4-11.

In Day 4 last week, we discussed the first part of this passage, focusing on the lack of spiritual growth or fruit in the Corinthians' lives. Here Paul addressed factions that had developed among the people of Corinth, no doubt as an extension of their spiritual immaturity.

Verse 4 discloses how the people seemed more focused on being followers of Paul or Apollos rather than on following the Lord Himself. In the verses that follow, Paul took them to task over their faulty thinking.

In verses 5-7 Paul clearly spelled out a minister's role. What is it?

In what way are we ministers in the lives of our sons?

Paul reminded the people that apart from God, they are nothing. Further, in teaching them about God, he and Apollos were simply fulfilling the task the Lord had given them.

Were Paul and Apollos assigned the same task? Explain.

While Paul and Apollos shared the same ultimate goal of planting and watering the seeds of God's salvation, they varied in style and approach.

What might this teach us about comparing ourselves to other Christian mothers whose parenting styles differ from our own?

One thing I've learned in this parenting journey is to reserve judgment when it comes to questioning the parenting styles of other Christian parents. I feel inadequate enough when it comes to my own parenting! Far be it for me to judge another mother for the way she handles the parenting challenges that come her way. Different people prefer different approaches to raising godly children, just as some of the Corinthians preferred Paul's teaching regarding how to live in relationship with God to the way Apollos presented the same message and basic principles. The important thing was their shared goal: pointing to Christ those who were entrusted to their care.

Write 1 Corinthians 3:7 here.

Circle who is responsible for growth in our sons' lives.

BRINGING IT home

Matthew Henry's Commentary notes, "The best qualified and most faithful ministers have a just sense of their own insufficiency, and are very desirous that God should have all the glory of their success."[17] We mothers are nothing more than gardeners who have been appointed the awesome privilege of planting and watering the seeds of God's life-changing truths in our sons' lives. That is the task assigned us—nothing more and nothing less.

Please hear me: At times our performance will fall short; other times we'll knock the ball out of the park. But regardless of our ups and downs, God alone is responsible for the outcome of our efforts. We are imperfect mothers raising imperfect sons in an imperfect world. As imperfect moms, we do our best to plant and water, relying all the while on a perfect God to bring the growth.

I realize that some women going through this study may feel dissatisfied with the way they've performed their assigned task (don't we all, at some level?), but let me encourage you to extend yourself some grace. Just as we can't expect our sons to grow up in the faith overnight, we too must understand that our spiritual growth happens over time. We moms are also works in progress.

In Philippians 1:6 Paul reminds and encourages us, "Being confident of this, that he who began a good work in you will carry it on to completion until the day of Christ Jesus" (NIV).

Read that verse aloud, but now replace the word *you* with "me."

Determine to believe the truth of that passage. As we grow up in the faith, our sons will feel the impact—even if the fruit is not yet evident.

WRAPPING IT up

What an honor to travel with you over the past five weeks of this study. We've covered quite a bit of ground and discussed some amazing biblical passages to aid us in the parenting journey. Your son is so blessed to have the kind of mother who will invest in his spiritual training. And even if he won't pat you on the back, I certainly will!

As we close, pray Philippians 1:6 for your boy. This time replace the word *you* with your son's name. Follow by asking God to give you the confidence in His ability to carry on the good work He began in your child's life. Allow me to close with the prayer I have for my own sons:

Heavenly Father,

I am sure of this, that He who started a good work in Ryan and Hayden will carry it on to completion until the day of Christ Jesus. Though not perfect, I commit myself to have the conversations in this book with my sons and to take advantage of teachable moments to point them to Your goodness and glory. I acknowledge that I cannot raise them to be godly in my own strength. I fully trust You for the results.

Thank You, Lord, for the awesome privilege of being Ryan and Hayden's mom! Amen.

TRAIN UP A CHILD

Where's the chart?

VIDEO GUIDE

These conversations are intended to be _____.
We're all works in progress.

A disturbingly high percentage of kids raised in church turn
their backs on faith.

_____ _____ _____ of all time:
Deuteronomy 6:4-9, NIV

> 4 "Hear, O Israel: The Lord our God, the Lord is one.
> 5 Love the Lord your God with all your heart and
>   with all your soul and with all your strength.
> 6 These commandments that I give you today are to be
>   upon your hearts.
> 7 Impress them on your children. Talk about them when
>   you sit at home and when you walk along the road,
>   when you lie down and when you get up.
> 8 Tie them as symbols on your hands and bind them
>   on your foreheads.
> 9 Write them on the doorframes of your houses
>   and on your gates."

A couple of takeaways from this passage sum up the charge
God has given us as mothers.

Our primary _____ _____ _____:
Raise kids who love God with their heart, soul, mind, and strength.

VIDEO GUIDE

1. ____ _____ _____ _____. We are to love the Lord our God with our heart, soul, mind, and strength.

Are we modeling something else as more important?

Love: *aw-hab´*; "to have affection for."

Where we place God in our order of affections will have greater influence on our children than any other form of Christian discipleship.

2. We are called to be the _____ _____ of our sons (vv. 7-9).

Phylactery contained four key passages, one of which was Deuteronomy 6.
Purpose: _____ of their covenant with God.

3. We disciple as we go, _____ _____ _____ in our children's lives.

If we are faithful in tending to our hearts, making sure that our primary affection is for the Lord, then our kids will catch that.

Remember the cross (RTC).
Be good because of what _____ _____ _____ (Rom. 5:8).

CONVERSATION STARTERS with your group:

What, if anything, consumes your time or your family's attention more than God?

Interested in reviewing this or other 5 Conversations Bible study sessions?
You can download all digital sessions by going to www.lifeway.com/women

BORN AGAIN

Have you ever wondered what the phrase *born again* means? The Bible records that Jesus used the phrase in a conversation with a man named Nicodemus. Nicodemus approached Jesus at night. He was curious about Jesus and the kingdom of God.

Jesus told him: "Unless someone is born again, he cannot see the kingdom of God" (John 3:3). Nicodemus responded, "But how can anyone be born when he is old?" (John 3:4).

Nicodemus was a highly moral man who obeyed God's law. He was a respected leader of the Jewish community. No doubt he was a fine man. Yet something was lacking. Like Nicodemus, many people today confuse religion with new birth in Christ. Phrases like "I pray regularly" or "I believe there is a God" often are confused with a real new-birth experience.

New birth begins with the Holy Spirit convicting a person that the person is a sinner. Because of sin, we are spiritually dead. For this reason, spiritual birth, as Jesus described it, is necessary. God loves us and gives us spiritual birth when we ask Him for it.

The Bible says all persons are sinners (Romans 3:23). Jesus died on a cross and was raised from the dead to save sinners. To be born again means that a person admits to God that he or she is a sinner, repents of sin, believes in or trusts Christ, and confesses faith in Christ as Savior and Lord. Jesus told Nicodemus that everyone who believes in (places faith in) Christ would not perish (John 3:16). Jesus is the only One who can save us (John 14:6).

To believe in Jesus is to be born again. Confess your sins and ask Jesus right now to save you. "Everyone who calls on the name of the Lord will be saved" (Acts 2:21).

After you have received Jesus Christ into your life, share your decision with another person, and following Christ's example, ask for baptism by immersion in your local church as a public expression of your faith (Romans 6:4; Colossians 2:6).

ENDNOTES

week one

1. Day for Mothers [online] 2011 [cited March 2011]. Available from the Internet: http://www.dayformothers.com/mothers-day-quotes/mothers-influence.html
2. Quotations Book [online] 2007 [cited March 2011]. Available from the Internet: http://quotationsbook.com/quote/14580/#axzz1GaNJjGmz
3. H. D. M. Spence and Joseph S. Exell, eds. *The Pulpit Commentary*, II Kings (London and New York: Funk and Wagnalls Company, n.d.), 440.
4. Ibid.
5. James Strong, *A Concise Dictionary of the Words in the Greek Testament and The Hebrew Bible* (Bellingham, WA: Logos Research Systems, Inc., 2009).
6. C. Soanes and A. Stevenson, *Concise Oxford English Dictionary* 11th ed., (Oxford: Oxford University Press, 2004). 694.
7. Strong.
8. K. W. Osbeck, *Amazing Grace: 366 Inspiring Hymn Stories for Daily Devotions* (Grand Rapids, MI: Kregel Publications, 1990), 293.
9. John Eldredge, *Wild at Heart* (Nashville, TN: Thomas Nelson, 2001), 13.
10. Rick Johnson, *That's My Son* (Grand Rapids, MI: Revell, 2005), 49.
11. Eldredge, 13-14.
12. Ibid.
13. Strong.
14. Welcome to the Quote Garden [online] 2010 [cited March 2011]. Available from the Internet: http://www.quote-garden.com/mom-day.html
15. C. S. Lewis, *Present Concerns* (Boston, MA: Houghton Mifflin Harcourt, 2002), 13.
16. Spence and Exell, 418.
17. Ibid.

week two

1. Alfred, Lord Tennyson Quotes [online] 2010 [cited March 2011]. Available from the Internet: http://thinkexist.com/quotation/the_happiness_of_a_man_in_this_life_does_not/222601.html
2. Mark Twain Quotes [online] 2011 [cited March 2011]. Available from the Internet: http://www.brainyquote.com/quotes/quotes/m/marktwain128375.html
3. H.D.M. Spence and Joseph S. Exell, eds. *The Pulpit Commentary*, II Samuel, Vol 2 (London and New York: Funk and Wagnalls Company, n.d.), 276.
4. Quotations Book [online] 2007 [March 2011]. Available from the Internet: http://quotationsbook.com/quote/7927/#axzz1GrzKKNe5
5. Spence and Exell, II Samuel, Vol. 2, 271.
6. Ibid., 265.
7. Matthew Henry, *Matthew Henry's Complete Commentary on the Whole Bible*, Vol. III, Job–Song of Solomon (Peabody, MA: Hendrickson Publishers, 1996), 217.
8. Quotations Book [online] 2007 [March 2011]. Available from the Internet: http://quotationsbook.com/quote/30617/#axzz1GrzKKNe5
9. Strong's Numbers, "epithumia." Available from the Internet: http://strongsnumbers.com/greek/1939.htm
10. Joseph Henry Thayer, *Thayer's Greek-English Lexicon of the New Testament* (Peabody, MA: Hendrickson Publishers, 1996).
11. Benjamin Franklin Quotes [online] 2010 [cited March 2011]. Available from the Internet: http://thinkexist.com/quotation/he_that_lies_down_with_dogs_shall_rise_up_with/146061.html
12. 60,000 Quotations [online] n.d. [cited March 2011]. Available from the Internet: http://myfamousquotes.com/?qid=10046
13. Spence and Exell, eds. *The Pulpit Commentary*, II Samuel, Vol 2, 272.
14. Walter L. Baker, Roy B. Zuck, Craig Blaising, *The Bible Knowledge Commentary: Old Testament* (David C. Cook, 1985), 468.
15. Mary Pickford Quotes [online] 2010 [cited March 2011]. Available from the Internet: http://thinkexist.com/quotes/mary_pickford/
16. Henry, Vol. II, Joshua to Esther, 497.

week three

1. Plato Quotes [online] 2010 [cited March 2011]. Available from the Internet: http://thinkexist.com/quotation/abstinence_is_the_surety_of/194255.html
2. Otis Ray Bowen Quotes [online] n.d. [cited March 2011]. Available from the Internet: http://www.finestquotes.com/author_quotes-author-Otis%20Ray%20Bowen-page-0.htm
3. "Should I feel terrible for being a 21 year old male virgin?" [online] n.d. [cited March 2011]. Available from the Internet: http://www.girlsaskguys.com/Sexuality-Questions/248240-should-i-feel-terrible-for-being-a-21-year-old.html
4. David B. Larson, MD, NMSPH, et al, "The Costly Consequences of Divorce: Assessing the Clinical, Economic, and Public Health Impact of Marital Disruption in the United States" (National Institute for Healthcare Research, Rockville, Maryland,1994, 84-85.
5. "Many Teens Regret Having Sex" [online] June 2000 [cited March 2011]. Available from the Internet: http://www.icrsurvey.com/Study.aspx?f=NatCam_Teens_Regret.html
6. Edmund T. Eddings, "Sexual Health Care: It's Important for Guys, Too" [online] 2007 [cited March 2011]. Available from the Internet: http://www.mtv.com/onair/ffyr/protect/sexetc_january.jhtml
7. 1 in 4 teen girls has sexually transmitted disease" [online] 2008 [cited March 2011]. Available from the Internet: http://www.msnbc.msn.com/id/23574940/
8. Pam Stenzel, *Sex Has a Price Tag: Discussions about Sexuality, Spirituality and Self-Respect* (Grand Rapids, MI: Zondervan,©2003), 51.

9. Ibid.

10. Sharon Jayson in *USA Today*, January 26, 2010 "Truth about sex: 60% of young men, teen boys lie about it" [online] January 26, 2010 [cited April 2011]. Available from the Internet: *http://www.usatoday.com/news/health/2010-01-26-boysandsex_ST_N.htm*

11. Ibid.

12. Joseph Henry Thayer, *Thayer's Greek-English Lexicon of the New Testament* (Peabody, MA: Hendrickson Publishers, 1996).

13. Joe S. McIlhaney and Freda McKissic Bush, *Hooked* (Chicago, IL: Northfield Publishers, 2008), 14.

14. Ibid., 14-15.

15. Ibid.,15.

16. Stenzel, 22.

17. John F. Walvoord, Roy B. Zuck, *The Bible Knowledge Commentary: An Exposition of the Scriptures* (Wheaton, IL: Victor Books, 1983).1025.

18. Famous Quotes About [online] n.d. [cited March 2011]. Available from the Internet: *http://www.famousquotesabout.com/quote/Anybody-who-believes-that/45082*

19. Gary J. and Carrie Oliver, *Raising Sons and Loving It! Helping Your Boys Become Godly Men* (Grand Rapids, MI: Zondervan Publishing House, 2000), 64.

20. Oliver, 66.

21. Rick Johnson, *That's My Son* (Grand Rapids, MI: Revell, 2005), 68.

22. Ibid., 66.

23. Thayer.

24. Ibid.

25. Ibid.

26. Harry S. Truman Quotes [online] 2010 [cited March 2011]. Available from the Internet: *http://thinkexist.com/quotation/in_reading_the_lives_of_great_men-i_found_that/147029.html*

27. Hanna Rosin, "Even Evangelical Teens Do It," [online] May 30, 2007 [cited March 2011]. Available from the Internet: *http://www.slate.com/id/2167293/.*

28. Ibid.

29. Diana Jean Schemo, *The New York Times*: "Study Finds Mothers Unaware of Children's Sexual Activity" [online] (September 2002] [cited March 2011]. Available from the Internet: *http://www.nytimes.com/2002/09/05/national/05SEX.html*

30. James Strong, *Strong's Greek Dictionary of the New Testament* (Nashville, TN: Thomas Nelson Publishers, 1996).

31. Franklin P. Jones Quotes [online] 2001 [cited April 2011]. Available from the Internet: *http://www.brainyquote.com/quotes/quotes/f/franklinp157131.html*

32. Patricia J. Dittus and James Jaccard, "Adolescents' Perceptions of Maternal Disapproval of Sex: Relationship to Sexual Outcomes," *Journal of Adolescent Health* 26, No. 4 (April 2000): 268-278.

33. Baptist Press, "Two-thirds of teens who had sex wish they had waited" [online] 2003 [cited April 2011]. Available from the Internet: *http://www.bpnews.net/bpnews.asp?ID=17294.*

34. *Millenials Rising: the next great generation*, in Vicki Courtney, *5 Conversations You Must Have with Your Daughter* (Nashville: B&H Publishing Group, 2009), 159.

35. University of Minnesota, "Closeness to Mother Can Delay Sexual Activity in Younger Teens" [online] n.d. [cited April 2011]. Available from the Internet: *http://mentalhealth.about.com/library/sci/0902/blteensex902.htm*

36. Schemo, *http://www.nytimes.com/2002/09/05/national/05SEX.html*

37. Baptist Press, *http://www.bpnews.net/bpnews.asp?ID=17294*

week four

1. Quotes on Childhood, [online] n.d. [cited April 2011]. Available from the Internet: *http://www.notable-quotes.com/c/childhood_quotes.html*

2 John F. Walvoord, Roy B. Zuck, *The Bible Knowledge Commentary: An Exposition of the Scriptures* (Wheaton, IL: Victor Books, 1983). 1331.

3. Meg Meeker, *Boys Should Be Boys: 7 Secrets to Raising Healthy Sons* (Washington, D.C., Regnary Publishing, 2008). 181.

4. Leonard Sax, *Boys Adrift* (New York: Basic Books, 2007), 142-143.

5. H.D.M. Spence and Joseph S. Exell, eds. *The Pulpit Commentary*, II Samuel, Vol 2 (London and New York: Funk and Wagnalls Company, n.d.).

6. Sax, 8-9.

7. Ibid, 9.

8. Lev Grossman, "Grow Up? Not So Fast" [online] January 16, 2005 [cited April 2011]. Available from the Internet: *http://www.time.com/time/magazine/article/0,9171,1018089-9,00.html#ixzz0tUmEBnvj*

9. Martin Luther Quotes [online] 2010 [cited April 2011]. Available from the Internet: *http://thinkexist.com/quotation/there_is_no_more_lovely-friendly-and_charming/150795.html*

10. Belinda Luscombe, "Who Needs Marriage? A Changing Institution" [online] November 18, 2010 [cited April 2011]. Available from the Internet: *http://www.time.com/time/nation/article/0,8599,2031962,00.html*

11. Lauren Frayer, "Poll: 4 in 10 Say Marriage Becoming Obsolete: [online] November 18, 2010 [cited April 2011]. Available from the Internet: *http://www.aolnews.com/2010/11/18/poll-4-in-10-say-marriage-becoming-obsolete/*

12. Albert Mohler, "The Case Against Marriage" [online] June 25, 2010 [cited April 2011]. Available from the Internet: *http://www.albertmohler.com/2010/06/25/the-case-against-marriage-courtesy-of-newsweek/*

13. "Social Indicators of Marital Health and Well-Being." In the 1976–1980 period, 73 percent of boys and 82 percent of girls said they expected to marry (or were already married); by 2001–2004, the boys' percentage jumped to 77 and the girls' to 84.5. [cited April 2011]. Available from the Internet: *http://www.stateofourunions.org/2010/si-teen_attitudes.php#fn2*

14. "Marital Status and health: US 1999-2002," Report from Center for Disease Control (2004). Interviews of 127,545 adults ages 18 up, found married adults in better psychological and physical health than cohabiting, single, or divorced adults.

15. "Sex Without Strings, Relationships Without Rings: Today's Young Singles Talk About Mating and Dating," [online] 2000 [cited April 2011]. Available from the Internet: *http://www.virginia.edu/marriageproject/pdfs/print_sexwithoutstrings.pdf*

16. Ibid.

17. Ibid.

18. Meeker. 173.

19. James Dobson Quotes [online] [cited April 2011] Available from the Internet: *http://thinkexist.com/quotation/don-t_marry_the_person_you_think_you_can_live/202882.html*

20. "The States of Marriage and Divorce," Pew Research Center [online] 2009 [cited April 2011]. Available from the Internet: *http://pewresearch.org/pubs/1380/marriage-and-divorce-by-state*

21. Late Dates: The dangerous art of marital procrastination; by Marcia Segelstein; Salvo; Issue 8 Spring 2009; *http://www.salvomag.com/new/articles/salvo8/8segelstein.php*

22. Ibid.

23. Albert Mohler; August 19, 2005; *http://www.albert-mohler.com/2005/08/19/what-if-there-are-no-adults-3/*; original quote is by Frederica Mathewes-Green; essay is published in "First Things;" August/September, 2005; *http://www.firstthings.com/*

24. Ibid.

25. "Late Dates: The dangerous art of marital procrastination."

26. Ibid.

27. "Sex Without Strings, Relationships Without Rings: Today's Young Singles Talk About Mating and Dating."

28. Pamela Smock, a demographer at the University of Michigan, says about 70 percent of those who get married lived together first. Cited in *5 Conversations You Must Have with Your Daughter* (Nashville: B&H Publishing Group), 195.

29. "Sex Without Strings, Relationships Without Rings: Today's Young Singles Talk About Mating and Dating."

30. "Seven Reasons Why Living Together Before Marriage is Not a Good Idea" [online] n.d. [cited April 2011]. Available from the Internet: *http://208.79.68.172/omf/marriage-ministry/7ReasonWhy.htm*

31. Ibid.

32. Ibid.

33. "Sociological Reasons Not to Live Together from All About Cohabiting Before Marriage" [online] 2010 [cited April 2011]. Available from the Internet: *http://www.leaderu.com/critical/cohabitation-socio.html*

34. Ibid.

35. Christian Quotes [online] n.d. [cited April 2011]. Available from the Internet: *http://christian-quotes.ochristian.com/christian-quotes_ochristiancgi?find=Christian-quotes-by-Charles+Spurgeon-on-Church*

36. Walvoord, Zuck, 793.

37. First Corinthians 3, *Matthew Henry's Complete Commentary on the Whole Bible* [online] n.d. [cited April 2011]. Available from the Internet: *http://www.biblestudytools.com/commentaries/matthew-henry-complete/1-corinthians/3.html*

week five

1. Michael Catt, *Courageous Living* (Nashville, TN: B&H Publishing Group, 2011), 81, forthcoming.

2. James Strong, A *Concise Dictionary of the Words in the Greek Testament and The Hebrew Bible* (Bellingham, WA: Logos Research Systems, Inc., 2009).

3. Benjamin Franklin Quotes [online] 2010 [cited April 2011]. Available from the Internet: *http://thinkexist.com/quotation/it_takes_many_good_deeds_to_build_a_good/184532.html*

4. The Quotations Page [online] 2010 [cited April 2011]. Available from the Internet: *http://www.quotationspage.com/quote/2871.html*

5. Strong.

6. Charles Kingsley Quotes [online] 2010 [cited April 2011]. Available from the Internet: *http://thinkexist.com/quotation/some_say_that_the_age_of_chivalry_is_past-that/260535.html*

7. Sindya Bhanoo, "How the Men Reacted as the Titanic and Lusitania Went Under" [online] March 1, 2010 [cited April 2011]. Available from the Internet: *http://www.nytimes.com/2010/03/02/science/02ships.html*

8. Jeffrey Kluger, "Titanic vs. Lusitania: How People Behave in a Disaster" [online] March 3, 2010 [cited April 2011]. Available from the Internet: *http://www.time.com/time/health/article/0,8599,1969142,00.html#ixzz0uRMBuRoJ*

9. Ibid.

10. Ibid.

11. Albert Mohler, "Women and Children First? A Tale of Two Ships" [onine] March 5, 2010 [cited April 2011]. Available from the Internet: *http://www.albertmohler.com/2010/03/05/women-and-children-first-a-tale-of-two-ships/*

12. Encyclopedia Titanica [online] 2010 [cited April 2011]. Available from the Internet: *http://www.encyclopedia-titanica.org/titanic-biography/john-harper.html*

13. Charles Spurgeon Quotes [online] 2010 [cited April 2011]. Available from the Internet: *http://thinkexist.com/quotation/humility_is_to_make_a_right_estimate_of_one-s/201144.html*

14. Kent Crockett, *Making Today Count for Eternity* (Sisters, OR: Multnomah Publishers, 2001), 122.

15. Strong.

16. Quotes and Notes [online] 2011 [cited April 2011]. Available from the Internet: *http://www.wholesome-words.org/echoes/sundaysays.html*

17. Matthew Henry, *Matthew Henry's Complete Commentary on the Whole Bible*, Vol. VI: Acts to Revelation (Peabody, MA: Hendrickson Publishers, 1996), 517.

LEADER GUIDE

by Bethany McShurley

The suggestions that follow will help you guide six sessions (75-90 minutes each) of *5 Conversations You Must Have with Your Son: The Bible Study*. Be willing to adapt these ideas to your group dynamic and join with God as He uses your group sessions for His glory.

Pray for the Lord's guidance in all aspects of this study, and ask your prayer partners to do the same. Encourage participants to enlist prayer support.

In advance, take care of all logistics. Reserve a meeting place, and secure a DVD player and a TV. Locate session supplies such as note cards and pens. Enlist a volunteer to provide healthful snacks if desired. Make sure your equipment works ahead of time! Work with church leaders to order resources.

If possible, arrange childcare during the study and highlight this benefit in your advertising. Send promotional postcards to all the moms in your church whose sons are preschool to college age. Use the church promotional segment on DVD 1.

Two weeks before your first meeting, post colorful flyers at church and possibly in the community. Use social media to get your message out. Be sure your event is announced at church. Use promotional downloads at *www.lifeway.com/women* to help get the word out.

This is an ideal study for meetings in neighborhood homes. If multiple groups are scheduled, help interested moms know about the different locations and times.

Session 1
INTRODUCTION and CONVERSATION 1
"Don't define manhood by the culture's wimpy standards. It's OK to be a man!"

In Advance

Provide modeling clay for each participant and images or items that represent common male roles: *businessman*, *cowboy*, *hunter*, *athlete*, and *soldier*. Also locate tasteful ads that suggest how male success comes through wealth accumulation, education, or relationships.

Welcome moms, introduce yourself, and ask each woman to share her name and the names/ages of her son(s).

What do you enjoy most about parenting a boy? What do you most hope to get out of this study?

Emphasize that the group's goal is not to focus on imperfections but to grow in dependence on Christ and to bring up our sons to be more like Him.

Talk About

Display images and ask volunteers to select some that come to mind when they hear the word *masculinity*. Explain how important it is for our sons to know what it really means to be a man—and that the answer isn't found in a career or in how many "toys" he accumulates.

How do you think most young men define manhood?

Scripture stands as the true authority on what it means to be a man. In this study women will better understand God's definition of manhood and how to help their sons rise to the challenge.

These goals will be accomplished through:
• home study
• Vicki's DVD teaching
• group discussion
• mutual support and friendship

View

Explain how Vicki previews each conversation on video and how we unpack it during the week. Move to her teaching of Conversation 1 (DVD and viewer guide, p. 9).

Debrief: *Scripture is filled with accounts of men who lived courageously and shadowed God's image. Raising such men requires intentionality.* Encourage each mom to gently shape her clay into a heart shape. *Just as we mold clay, so do we also shape our sons' moral and spiritual lives to align with God's design.*

What qualities do you think God desires to see in young men? (See Mic. 6:8; Matt. 22:36-39)

How would love, justice, and mercy influence our sons' work? marriages? parenting?

Acquaint women with the interactive elements on page 8. Comment: *Although it's difficult to imagine, God loves our sons more than we do. This Bible study will help us discover His truths and learn how to raise our sons accordingly.*

Support and Pray

Close in prayer, asking God to touch each mom's heart with a fresh love for her son(s) and to renew her commitment to be the best mom she can be with His help.

Remind the group to complete the Week 1 home study before the next group meeting. Ask moms to share e-mail addresses to stay in touch if they choose.

Session 2
CONVERSATION 2
"What you don't learn to conquer may become your master."

In Advance

Bring an extra cell phone and enlist a participant to portray your teenage son on the other end of the call. Spend a few minutes developing the script and timing based off the "View" activity. Encourage her to overact to emphasize the rudeness of taking a phone call and the pressure to lie.

Week 1 Review

Sessions 2-6 have options to review each week's home study. Or select your own questions from the workbook. (Watch your time if schedule is a consideration.) Here are options for helping your group review Week 1:

How does the idea of godly mothers serving as regents in their sons' lives impact your interactions with your son?

When you initially set goals for your son's future (see p. 12), were they more *worldly focused* or *spiritually focused*? Explain.

View

Move into Vicki's video teaching of Conversation 2 (DVD and viewer guide, p. 39).

Begin debriefing the DVD teaching, and then act startled as if a cell call is coming in. Apologetically pick up the phone and ask women to hold on for a moment. Turn away from the group, and begin a conversation as if with your teenage son, who is begging to go off campus for lunch one day. Let the call go on for a while to communicate the idea of mom being worn down.

To stop the pleading, finally agree to call the school and give the excuse that he has a doctor's appointment. On the other end, "he" acts excited and hangs up. End the call, looking frustrated. Begin to notice and interact with the group again.

Debrief: *What temptation did the son face? What about his mom? How could each issue become one of mastery and self-control? What example did she set?*

Our sons will be constantly confronted with temptation and teased when they don't cave. Self-control is the wise man's ally, even in what seems like small things. Otherwise, they turn into bigger, complicated issues of character.

Ask a volunteer to explain Vicki's S-T-P model for avoiding temptation.

Talk About

Option: Answer a Conversation Starter from the video viewer guide (p. 39).

Ask women to call out threats that might master their sons. Encourage participants to look for opportunities to teach their boys the S-T-P model. Act as the voice of reason for your sons until they are old enough to think things through on their own.

Storytelling has long been a vehicle for moral lessons; for example, Jesus' parables. Share a time when self-control protected you.

How might your son benefit by hearing your account of protection you have found in self-control?

Support and Pray

Take a note card for each one of your sons, writing his first and middle names. Pass cards to your right. Pray over the names you receive—that God would help the boys grow into young men who master their passions by relying on the Lord's help.

Session 3
CONVERSATION 3
"Not everyone's doing it!" (And other truths about sex you won't hear in the locker room.)

In Advance

Set up a card table with two facing chairs. At the top of one sheet of paper, write *God's View on Sexual Purity*; on another, *The Oxytocin Factor, Why It Matters*; and on a third, *Why Waiting Leads to Satisfaction*.

Week 2 Review

Sin is not a behavior but a condition. See "Plan of Salvation," page 160, and discuss how God offers a way out.

Why do you think moms should work to block their kids' pursuit of sinful pleasures?

View

Prior to beginning the DVD, ask ladies to number 1,2,3. Ask the 1s to take notes regarding God's views on sex. The 2s are to pay attention to the topic of oxytocin. Ask the 3s to listen for the value of waiting.

Continue with Vicki's teaching of Conversation 3 (DVD and viewer guide, p. 69).

Talk About

Give each team one of the three tear sheets. Ask teams to brainstorm some talking points moms might use to help drive home assigned concepts.

Assign someone the role of a preteen son. Each team appoints a speaker to play "mom" in presenting the topic. Take turns sitting across from the boy and sharing the information. Overlap is OK. Keep things in good taste and encourage sincerity, but allow for humor.

Why should moms speak up on the topic of sex?

What's the value of having "the talk" more than once?

Support and Pray

Pray that God will give each mom confidence to hold ongoing communication with her son about sexual purity. Ask for blessing and guidance for any moms whose sons are in rebellion.

Session 4
CONVERSATION 4
"Boyhood is only for a season. P.S. It's time to grow up!"

Share a favorite memory of your sons playing superhero with these questions:

Why do you think so many little boys long to be powerful … someone to be "reckoned with"?

Why do you think God put that drive in the young male heart?

How does this drive carry over into adulthood? Explain.

Week 3 Review

Allow moms to share ways they took advantage of teachable moments last week in talking to their sons about sexual purity.

View

Move into Vicki's video teaching of Conversation 4 (DVD and viewer guide, p. 99).

Talk About

Across the top of a tear sheet, write *Peter Pan Who Shaves* and *A Man of Excellence*. Ask participants to list qualities they would expect to find in each category of men.

Ask moms to name one positive quality they see in their sons. Encourage them to point it out to their boys as something they do well.

What can we do to encourage our sons to become men of excellence?

Encourage: *Even if sons lack a godly male role model, they can still grow into strong leaders who please God.* Discuss setting behavioral expectations as well as achievable goals.

How might knowing what is expected of them before they leave our care help our sons better navigate life?

What expectations might we appropriately set for ages:

2-6?   **7-12?**

13-18?   **19-22?**

Support and Pray

Encourage moms to dedicate time this week to praying for their sons' future wives, as well as for their sons' sensitivity to God's leadership in their lives.

Session 5
CONVERSATION 5
"Godly men are in short supply—dare to become one!"

Week 4 Review

Ask moms to share how their attitude toward parenting is evolving. Continue encouraging them to stay the course.

What practical steps can we take to raise "top-shelf kinda guys," those who resist the pressure to conform and seek to live by God's standards?

Using Vicki's vintage motifs as a spinoff, contrast marriage today with marriage 50-100 years ago. Discuss ways to help sons view marriage as a blessing (and cohabitation as a risk and threat).

After responses, reassure: *If you've experienced brokenness or are rearing children after a breakup, know that God loves you, is willing to forgive, and wants you to move on in victory. No matter what lies in your past, your children are not destined to repeat your choices.*

The goal of parenting is to ground our children in God's truths so they will eventually seek Him on their own in all areas of life.

How can you serve as a "trainer" to help your son acquire and put discernment into practice?

View

Play Vicki's teaching of Conversation 5 (DVD and viewer guide, p. 127).

Talk About

Making our relationship with God a priority will strengthen our ability to parent with godly wisdom.

How do you let God know you are serious about giving Him full control of your life?

God is interested above all in the condition of our hearts.

What are some discipline ideas that highlight heart examination over behavioral modification?

What tools can we use/people can we enlist to reach this goal?

Support and Pray

Pray, asking God to help each mom view her life through His eyes—and to do whatever is necessary to help lead her son to Christ or strengthen his walk with Him.

Session 6
Train up a Child ... Where's the chart?

In Advance
Obtain salt packets for each participant, a children's bank, and a bag of coins.

Week 5 Review
List traits expected in a good peer.

What can we do to help our sons foster positive peer relationships? Why is this important?

Discuss the value of selflessness, and encourage women to share stories of how someone's self-sacrifice impacted them. Create a list of service activities through which young men can begin to experience personally the value of putting others first.

View
Conclude video teaching with Vicki's challenge to remain faithful in discipling their sons (DVD and viewer guide, pp. 158-59).

Talk About
Give each mother a salt packet as a reminder of these truths: *In Matthew 5:13 Jesus said that His followers are the "salt of the earth." Just as salt makes one seek water, so can Christian moms help their boys begin to thirst for God's truth.*

What practical steps might we take to help our sons thirst for God rather than the world?

Reinforce: *By helping our sons grow in knowledge and love for the Lord, we make holy deposits in their lives.*

Encourage participants as they suggest actions they can take to help sons develop a healthy respect for God. Hand out a coin for each suggestion, asking the speaker to drop her deposit into the bank.

Remind the group that while parents are their kids' primary disciplers, spiritual growth comes from the Lord. On a tear sheet, make two columns: *Trusting* and *Obsessing*. List behaviors associated with truly trusting God with our sons' futures, plus those that suggest a greater focus on our own efforts.

Support and Pray
Encourage moms to gather in groups of two to four each, to pray for continued strength and for God's protection and intervention in their sons' lives. Encourage mothers to set up recurring mom-son outings to stay engaged and in touch.

.mom
a lifeway women event

WITH WORSHIP BY   MELISSA GREENE

ANGELA THOMAS
PRISCILLA SHIRER
ANGIE SMITH, VICKI COURTNEY & MORE!

CONNECT WITH OTHER MOMS!
WORKSHOPS FROM ADOPTION TO ORGANIZATION

REGISTER TODAY
lifeway.com/dotmom   800.254.2022

Event subject to change without notice.

Five Conversations You Must Have

{ with daughters and sons! }

from author Vicki Courtney

AVAILABLE NOW

5 Conversations You Must Have with Your Son

1. Don't define manhood by the culture's wimpy standards; it's okay to be a man!
2. What you don't learn to conquer may become your master.
3. Not everyone's doing it! (And other truths about sex you won't hear in the locker room.)
4. Boyhood is only for a season. *P.S. It's time to grow up!*
5. Godly men are in short supply—dare to become one!

ISBN: 978-0-8054-4666-1
$14.99 // Paperback // 288 pgs.

5 Conversations You Must Have with Your Daughter

1. You are more than the sum of your parts
2. Don't be in such a hurry to grow up
3. Sex is great . . . and worth the wait
4. It's OK to dream about marriage and motherhood
5. Girls gone wild are a dime a dozen—dare to be virtuous

ISBN: 978-0-8054-4986-0
$14.99 // Paperback // 288 pgs.

B&H WOMEN
Substantive. Virtuous. Ra...
BHWomen.con

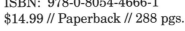

AVAILABLE NOW